AF247495

PREFACES

Lectures on Art Subjects

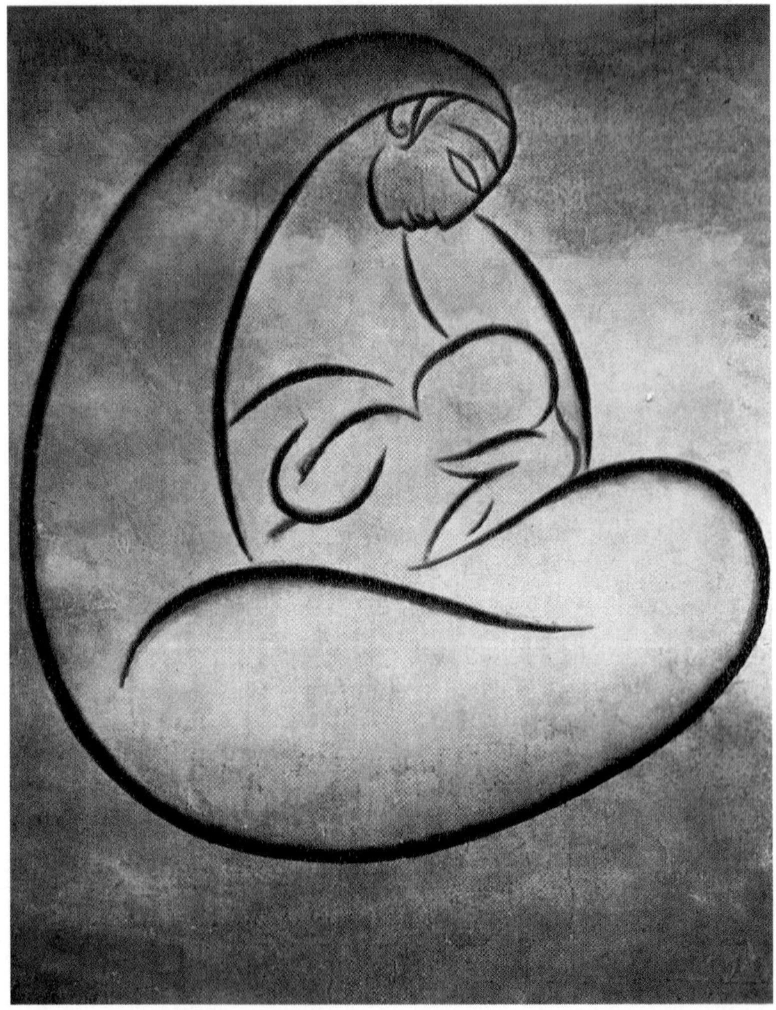

Mother and Child by Jamini Roy, 291/4" x 21". Courtesy Mathilde Andrée Rahim, Calcutta

PREFACES

Lectures on Art Subjects

SHAHID SUHRAWARDY

Introduction by
Naz Ikramullah Ashraf

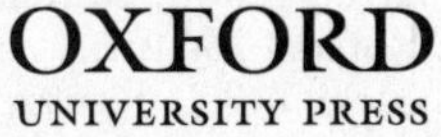

OXFORD
UNIVERSITY PRESS

OXFORD
UNIVERSITY PRESS

Great Clarendon Street, Oxford OX2 6DP

Oxford University Press is a department of the University of Oxford. It furthers the University's objective of excellence in research, scholarship, and education by publishing worldwide in

Oxford New York

Auckland Cape Town Dar es Salaam Hong Kong Karachi Kuala Lumpur Madrid Melbourne Mexico City Nairobi New Delhi Shanghai Taipei Toronto

with offices in

Argentina Austria Brazil Chile Czech Republic France Greece Guatemala Hungary Italy Japan Poland Portugal Singapore South Korea Switzerland Turkey Ukraine Vietnam

First published by Bhupendralal Banerjee at the Calcutta University Press, Senate House, Calcutta 1938.

ISBN 978-0-19-547671-2

This edition by Oxford University Press 2009

Typeset in Adobe Caslon Pro
Printed in Pakistan by
Kagzi Printers, Karachi.
Published by
Ameena Saiyid, Oxford University Press
No. 38, Sector 15, Korangi Industrial Area, PO Box 8214
Karachi-74900, Pakistan.

TO
MY FATHER

Contents

Introduction

Shahid Suhrawardy (1890–1965) was born in Midnapur, West Bengal and belonged to a family well known for their contribution to education, reform and public service. His mother Khujista Akhtar Banu Suhrawardia Begum, was one of the pioneering Muslim women of her generation, she was both multilingual and a scholar and translated books from English into Urdu. She was also the Examiner at Calcutta University of the work of Persian language scholars.

Today, Shahid Suhrawardy is regarded by Pakistani and Bangladeshi critics as the first *modern*, English Language poet of undivided India. He published his famous *Essays in Verse* in 1935. He was also a scholar, writer, and art critic and in his time he was admired for his vast knowledge of the arts. He has been described as a living legend because of his astonishing linguistic attainments and scholarly achievements but in spite of this he lived his life without ever promoting himself. Over the years, he became an academic whose astonishing knowledge and skills were known only to a select few.

Shahid Suhrawardy graduated from Calcutta University in 1908 and left for Europe the following year. He was at the Sorbonne in Paris from 1910 to 1911. He went on to study history and law at Oxford University. After his graduation in 1914 he left for Russia to study Slavic languages. He taught English language and literature at the Imperial University of St. Petersburg and the Women's University in Moscow. Amongst his students was Alexander Kerensky, the Prime Minister of Russia in 1917 shortly before the Bolshevik Revolution. He later helped Kerensky write his memoirs. Although Shahid Suhrawardy immersed himself in European culture and did not return to India for twenty years, this did not preclude him from looking at the arts of India and Asia. He was deeply interested in them all—painting, literature and the performing arts.

Shahid Suhrawardy was my mother's cousin, and for me, a very special person: He had a profound influence on my thinking. My earliest recollection is of him listening with my mother to the news of the Partition of India on the radio. This was in Calcutta in 1946. I also remember going with him for drives to Victoria Maidan in an open car. Later, in Pakistan, I remember him surrounded by friends, the centre of lively conversations, or ordering the most marvellous Chinese food from Mr Lee, the owner of the ABC restaurant in Karachi. This was always a great occasion! Eating with Shahid *Muma* was always a memorable experience because he was also a gourmet—he introduced me to Russian as well as Spanish and Greek food. Over the years I learnt that Shahid *Muma* had lived in Paris and before that in Russia, and that he had been working with Stanislavsky in Moscow Theatre before the communist revolution. We knew he spoke and read many languages, the European being English, German, French, Spanish, Italian, Russian, and Asian being Chinese, Urdu, Arabic and Persian, but he always said '*Mujhe to sirf dhai zabane ateen hein*' (I only know two-and-a-half languages).

On a visit to the Tate Gallery in London he once stood before the work of the artist Max Ernst and asked 'Is he alive or dead?' and then added 'His wife made a good *borscht*' (a Russian soup). This personal anecdote was how he enlivened his conversations. At the Chartres Cathedral in Paris with my parents and siblings he took me aside and showed me the sculptural figures on its façade explaining their importance in art because he knew I was studying art. To him above all, I owe my values, which gave me insights and sensitized me as an artist. He never thrust his great erudition at people but shared it with those who were truly interested—as I was. His advice to my parents was 'Let her look, send her to the major museums, and let her look'... to me he said 'beware *couleur locale*'—meaning don't paint village girls with *gharas* (earthen pots), or village views which had no relationship to my own life. He was pleased when he learnt that I admired the work of Matisse. He wrote in a book on Matisse which I purchased as a birthday gift from him, 'I pray you realize, dear Naz, in your life and art Matisse's rhythm—his musicality'.

He is credited with having 'discovered' the renowned artist Jamini Roy. The well known Bangladeshi artist Sultan spoke warmly of his encouragement. In Europe he had become friends with poets and writers such as Robert Bridges, D.H. Lawrence, and Robert Trevelyan of the British literary world. In Moscow he became involved with the Moscow Art Theatre and staged Rabindranath Tagore's *Raja* so successfully that he was appointed to the chair of joint *regisseur*. During this period he also worked with Stanislavsky. When the Bolshevik Revolution occurred he escaped to Berlin and later he worked at Prague University. From 1921 to 1928 he was one of the producers of the theatre and the expert (art section) of the International Institute of Intellectual Cooperation under the League of Nations in Paris. It was not surprising therefore, that he was part of the art advisory committee for the decoration of the first three buildings of the UNESCO headquarters in Paris in 1958.

On his return to undivided India, Shahid Suhrawardy became active in the cultural life of Calcutta. He was a contemporary of Malcolm Muggeridge, who was Editor of *The Statesman* and they became friends. He was appointed Bageshwari Professor of Indian Fine Arts in the department of ancient Indian history and culture. In the same year he became the Nizam Professor of Islamic culture and delivered a series of lectures at the Visva Bharati.

In 1938 his lectures on art were collected and published by Calcutta University. The book was called *Prefaces*. This includes one of the earliest appreciations of the artist Jamini Roy's work.

The topics are varied: Indian Art, Art and Education, Indo-Persian Painting, and Theatrical Art to name a few. In each essay he explores the historical influences found in the art form. We learn of Persian painting's influence on Rajasthani painting—

form, ideas, themes and style. When discussing art and education his statements are as fresh today as when they were written a little over 70 years ago. These essays are exciting to read. Few writers and critics give such cogent examples to back up their views.

The essay on theatrical art gives us the background to the development of the 'method school of acting' which originated in Russia under Stanislavsky. He compares this form of acting with the tradition of Russia and also compares it to the form of Indian theatre of the time.

In 'A Nation's Art' he discusses '*what are those objects produced by human endeavour that can be called works of art—in other words, why is the status of art accorded to a certain category of objects and denied to others*?' Art, literature and poetry are defined in the quest of art criticism. These lectures are a revelation in terms of our understanding of art generally and an education in the way one can establish parameters to formulate our own references for the future.

Though each essay is layered with information on many facets of the topic they are written in simple terms and make reading them an enjoyable experience whether one is an artist, art lover or educationist.

His many other books include *Of Mussalman Culture* by Vassili Vladimirovich Bartold which was translated by Suhrawardy into English from the Russian and published in 1934. From 1940 to 1947 he was the art critic for *The Statesman*. In 1948, he translated the poems Lee Hou Chee into English with the help of another Chinese poet. He was a member of undivided Bengal's public service commission and after Partition took up a similar post in Pakistan. In Pakistan he was the first head of PEN (Poets, Essayists and Novelists, a branch of the International organization) He also held the position of Professor of Oriental Art at Columbia University in the USA before becoming Pakistan's Ambassador to Spain, a position which he used to further his research on Spanish Islamic Arts.

The posthumous publication *The Art of the Mussulmans in Spain* was written as a series of lectures which were given in Calcutta in the 1930s. His phenomenal knowledge of languages and the arts makes reading *The Art of the Mussulmans in Spain* a veritable feast—it is a unique example of the writing of history and inter-cultural influences unaffected by biases of any kind. History and anecdotal stories are so well woven that one is amused and informed at the same time.

Suhrawardy has indeed left behind a rich legacy for future generations.

Naz Ikramullah Ashraf

PREFACES

LECTURES ON ART SUBJECTS

SHAHID SUHRAWARDY

Rani Bageshwari Professor of Fine Arts & Fellow,
Calcutta University
Sometime Reader in English Literature,
Imperial University & Women's University, Moscow

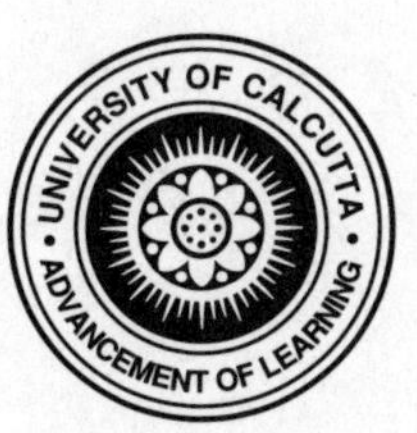

AT THE UNIVERSITY PRESS
CALCUTTA

Foreword

Most of these papers are lectures read out by me to students at various intervals at the Osmania University, Hyderabad, the Visvabharati, the Lucknow Exhibition, c.1936 (Fine Arts Pavilion), and at other places. Three of them are condensed and recalled from talks given at the London BBC and at the Calcutta station of the All-India Radio.

My heart-felt thanks are due to Mr Syamaprasad Mookerjee, Vice-Chancellor, Calcutta University, for the consideration and encouragement I have always received at his hands as well as to Mr Jogeschandra Chakravorti, our Registrar, for the extreme kindness and courtesy he has always shown me. I wish also to record my appreciation of the help kindly rendered by the staff of the University Press, particularly by Mr Kalipada Das, the Superintendent, who took the trouble of going through the final proofs, and by my friend, Mr Bhupendralal Banerjee, the University Printer, whose unfailing patience I am afraid I much tried during the accelerated printing of this book.

I am also grateful to Madame Mathilde Andrée Rahim, Mr Apurvakumar Chanda and Mrs Grace Clarke, the painter, for allowing me to reproduce here pictures by Jamini Roy, which are in their possession. Jamini Roy himself gave me much of his valuable time in looking through the proofs and controlling the colours. All the blocks have been printed by the Indian Photo Engraving Coy., Calcutta. The half-tone blocks of the *Mother and Child* and the coloured one of *A Woman's Face* were also executed there. The block of *Rama, Lakshman and Sita* is the property of the Prabartak Publishing Coy., and was kindly lent me by them. The cloth on the book is of Bengal, hand-woven and hand-spun here.* I wish to pay a tribute to Mr J.K. Biswas,

---

* This refers to the original book.

whose firm is responsible for the binding, for his forbearance towards me as well as for having helped me to introduce an innovation in University publications, which I hope the authorities will see their way to adopt.

I take this opportunity of particularly thanking my friends Apurvakumar Chanda and Tulsichandra Goswami for having suggested several improvements in the text, all of which I gladly accepted. They spent many fatiguing hours whilst I read out long passages to them from this book, and their interest in it and anxiety on my account are yet another proof, if proof were needed, of that deep, and I hope lasting, friendship which links me with them.

I must also mention my uncle, Sir Hassan Suhrawardy, a former Vice-Chancellor, whose helpful solicitude in whatever work I undertake has been a source of strength to me, although I have always felt that his faith in me is based more on affection than on my merits.

In conclusion, I must express here my unabating sense of gratitude to the gentlest of friends and teachers, Maria Nikolaevna Germanova, the well-known tragic actress, and Aleksandr Petrovich Kalitinsky, formerly Professor at the Imperial Archaeological Institute of Moscow and sometime Director of the Institut Kondakovianum at Prague, from whom I learnt many of the values which obtain not only in art but also in life.

I am happy that even a work of such slight content, as this small book is, should necessitate acknowledgements to so many good and gifted men and women.

Senate House,
Calcutta University.
1938

1

On the Study of Indian Art*

I am grateful to you for the honour you have done me in electing me to preside over the Fine Arts Section of this Conference. I take it as a compliment not to me personally but to my University, which is the only educational institution in India to have realised that the fine arts are a sufficiently important subject to be included in the curriculum of its postgraduate studies. By establishing a chair and uniting together a number of scholars, the late Sir Asutosh Mookerjee, with characteristic vision, gave concrete form to the growing desire for a deeper understanding of this aspect of ancient Indian culture. Thereby the dignity of a discipline has been conferred on this subject which, till lately, used to be the special sphere of sentimental exaltation of the dilettante and effete appreciation of the aesthete.

Today I wish to draw your attention to some problems that I consider of paramount importance for the study of the history of Indian fine arts and I intend to appraise for you the methods that have been employed till now in the field of its investigation. I assure you that my criticism is inspired by a genuine desire to clarify as best I can the confusion prevailing on the subject, and not by hostility or prejudice towards the pioneers of our studies whose attempts I would be the last to undervalue. In this address I shall try to suggest a different approach and, because of this, I shall be compelled to diverge from the views of many for whom I have admiration and feelings of gratitude.

---

* Delivered at the eighth session of the All-India Oriental Conference at Mysore in December 1935.

For so long had it been the custom to belittle the achievements of Indian culture and characterise them as expressions of crudity and the grotesque, that it is quite intelligible if, at the beginning, the reaction was of an unscientific and uncritical nature. Thus, when everything was considered unworthy and as belonging to a low rung of cultural existence, the writers, who might be called the discoverers of our art, went to the other extreme of finding each art object in India to be supremely valuable and significant. This reactive hostility towards superficial comparisons with European classical and modern art led them to appreciate art objects not for their intrinsic worth but as elements in the fight for national culture. It is not the first time that this has occurred; in the history of the world this uncritical over-praise of mediocre expressions of culture is an oft-recurring phenomenon. The pity is that so much emotion and fine writing has been wasted in refuting the untenable and prejudiced arguments of our opponents.

A little more knowledge on our part, for instance, of the beginnings of Early Christian art, not to speak of the existing folk art of eastern and northern Europe, would have been sufficient to oppose a propaganda spread by supercilious and untrained foreigners. The truth is that those critics who denied the validity of Indian art were either ignorant, or else were devoid of that deep cultural adaptability essential to the visual apprehension of unusual forms. The more serious among them found the manifestations of our art strange. The average European normally reacts thus to any art with a history or inspiration different to his own. We would probably have done the same if of late our taste had not been enslaved by alien ideals. A feeling of 'strangeness' in the presence of an art object is no stigma attached to that object but a confession of the incapacity of the observer to adjust his sensibility to it. Need we in our turn have taken the absurd position of maintaining that everything created in India was beyond criticism, of tearing out from our hearts all joy in foreign art, even while it evoked the deepest aesthetic reaction, denying artistic excellence, for example, to classical Greece and Italy and France during and after the middle ages? Was it right to regard Indian art as an insular, narrow, specific, harboured but all-justifiable instance of a particular mode of artistic existence? Why should it have been necessary to insist upon a special initiation into the mysteries of an esoteric culture as an essential equipment for the understanding of Indian art? In refusing a generality of appeal to western art they have robbed our own art, which is one of the most marvellous expressions of the human spirit, of that element which alone justifies the existence of art. However, we must admit that, embittered though they were with a sense of inferiority, these writers have served a useful purpose in gaining publicity for our art and in clearing the ground which, for want of a national cultural criterion, had lain encumbered with overgrowths for centuries.

The second method of studying our subject confused the issues if possible still more. This was the 'aesthetic' method and it has not yet disappeared, if we are to judge from the great volume of writing on fine arts today. In fact, for the last thirty years almost every historian of our art has been guilty of exhausting the English vocabulary of adjectives denoting beauty and excellence to apply to it. There are few books or articles where, after the metric description has been given of an art object, it is not at once characterised as exquisite, graceful, fine, beautiful. How is it possible that, in what is a comparatively ample corpus today, in spite of the absence of excavations on a comprehensive scale, the ravages of time and the vandalism of man, all examples can be described as perfect or even excellent? The followers of this school pretend to guard with zeal the isolation of their subject from cognate and allied disciplines. The word archaeology is anathema to them. They prefer to connect art with literature, religion, meditation, with lyrical outpourings on legends and mythology. You will find a large number of books which, filled with emotional effusion of the most uncritical kind, contain the narration *in extenso* of the subject-matter of works of art that are identified with stories from the jatakas, the Krishna legends and historical episodes. It would seem that to these writers the sole purpose of art was illustration. I do not deny that the illustrative quality, besides being an indication of the adequacy of technique to a theme, is perhaps also an element in our intellectual acceptance of a work of art. It helps us to understand in what particular way a certain object has been refracted in the mind of the artist and exteriorised to our visuality; but you will agree with me that, however interesting this might be on other counts, the illustrative quality plays but a meagre part in our final judgment of art objects. Indeed, it is the least important factor at the moment when we contemplate a work of art in terms of its composition, the rightful apprehension of which constitutes the only basis of art criticism. With the lapse of time the illustrative quality is the first to evaporate from our memory, whilst we still retain some recollections of linear inter-relations, structure, modelling, plan, colours, disposition of masses in space,—in short, of the arrangement and of the resultant radiance which reflect the union of the artist's brain and his emotional sensibility with his material.

Now let us examine the attitude of this school towards archaeology. I admit that an approach which consists in regarding art objects as mere utilitarian elements in material culture cannot commend itself to art historians. I yield to no one in upholding the autonomy and integrity of our subject. But to me the wholesale condemnation of archaeology in our present state of knowledge of Indian art appears to be childish, capricious and fanatical. From the point of view of method, the importance of archaeology for our subject must be rightly appraised, always, of course, bearing in mind the clear line which demarcates the aims of these two disciplines. I too would have liked to dispense with archaeology, if it were possible. But can we afford to indulge in this luxury when the greater portion of our art still awaits excavation? This dependence on archaeology is not only our lot but that of the students of all the classical arts except the Hellenic. There the entire corpus, or much the largest portion of it, has been unearthed, all the literary documents sifted, the chronology elucidated, the reigning ideas discovered, the historical episodes brought to light, and thus it is possible to review the whole range of the artistic achievement of the Hellenic peoples and trace not only the influences and counter-influences but the rise, the growth, the culmination and the dissipation of forms and technique. Only in that unique instance can we ignore archaeology, and that for the sole reason that it has already contributed its full to art history. In our case you will admit the objection is unreasonable. In fact, those who are most vociferous in decrying this inevitable alliance rely in their own works on literary allusions, customs, history, etc., which more rightly belong to the sphere of archaeological investigation. I for one, if it came to that, would prefer that our books be loaded with unilluminated archaeological material rather than with subjective exclamations serving as confessions of the writer's personal aesthetic reactions. This is an interesting enough theme in the autobiographies of art historians, who have risen to eminence as great human beings; otherwise they are devoid of any value. Art history does not consist in recording the aesthetic sensibility of all and sundry who choose to write on art. There is so much of loose thinking and writing on this subject that I have deemed it a duty to expatiate on it at some length.

The third school is that of the 'idealists.' Their method emphasises the idealism, chiefly religious, underlying Indian art. It is an attempt, in the last analysis, to divert our attention from the quality of uniqueness inherent in every art object towards generalisations dealing with the psychological equipment of the creative artist. Their interpretation thus is in terms of the content rather than of the form. You will have recognised that this approach is the most popular with the majority of our serious art historians. I hope you realise the grave dangers of such an attitude. It presupposes, in spite of the growing evidence we have from day to day of the stupendous material achievements of ancient Indian culture, religious idealism to have been the unique interest of the Indian spirit. It proceeds further and holds, as logically it must, that all the phases of our life are explicable only with reference to a special kind of spiritual outlook, which is our sole monopoly. To explain away what to alien eyes appear extravagances of our art, it contrasts the spirituality of our culture with the so-called materialism of the West. All the disturbing discrepancies of our history it attributes to the irrelevancy of foreign contacts, not taking into account the need for other than spiritual activity that magnificent military empires and luxurious courts must have had, where the patrons of art often regarded religion either as a social convenience or as a factor in national cohesion. They would have us believe that the ordinary man in Ancient India lived his everyday life in primitive simplicity and goodness. Artists to them were not only god-gifted but god-drunk. Surely, an artist cannot be judged by his passionate love of god, or even by his elevated theme, but only by his realisation of that theme in form. He must have the vision, the technical prowess and knowledge of the nature of his material as well as of the limitations of the human creative capacity. He may be the devotee of a particular creed but he must be something more. He is not worthy of his appellation if, for the purpose of his creation, he is solely dependent on iconographical tradition. Even when the artist follows traditions he exercises his choice among different sets of tradition. He must be sensitive to the changes of taste that take place even in countries where conventions are supposed to be immutable. His search, whatever be his theme, must always be the same, *viz.*, after vitality, glamour and expressiveness. The question is whether, at the miraculous moment of creation, he is the idealised man who has gained a vision of truth by meditation, prayer and atonement or is he also alive to commercial advantages, the vision being revealed to him in the process of the work through the urge of his temperament? We talk too much of the sacredness of our conventions and traditions, yet Indian art has the supreme merit, in spite of the apparent lack of variety of its themes, of having successfully avoided in its best products the academism into which other hieratic arts, for example the Babylonian and some phases of the Egyptian and the Byzantine, so easily fall. In fact, for a longer period than any other people of the classical East, we have, through changing ages and dynasties, maintained a higher standard of originality, vividness and efficiency until, late in our history, we lapsed into formalism and the baroque.

Another claim which the 'idealists' make for Indian art is its collective aspect which they contrast with the anarchy of individual expression in the West. I take this to mean that whilst the Indian artist was a faithful mirror to the ideals of the collective to which he belonged, the European created forms in response to an impulse which was all his own. Thus it would result that, whilst the Indian was secure against criticism and sure of receiving a certain measure of standardised appreciation, the European was exposed to adventitious subjective reactions. Is this view really tenable in the light of our knowledge? Does it not tend to reduce the Indian creative genius to something mechanical, meek and submissive? Does not the pathos of Indian art controvert this supposition? The anonymity of our artists, so often cited to support this theory, does not signify their abdication from the vanity of personal creation. Can it not allude to an extraordinary objectivity in art appreciation which ancient Indian society had achieved, an objectivity which consisted in completely divorcing the product of art from the personality of its producer? Moreover, anonymity has been to a large extent a characteristic of all aspects of our cultural life. The practice is common enough in other civilizations of a teleological type, whether Asiatic or European. We cannot too strongly refute this supposition which denies freedom to the Indian artist and seeks to portray him as an automaton in our culture. In reality he is neither bound hand and foot by iconographical traditions nor is he that rare phenomenon, a pure artist without admixture of artisanship, independent of the hazards of creation. We must for the sake of the dignity of the Indian artist reinvest him with the characteristics of human weakness. Neither can we scientifically accept the view of this school, which would reduce the manifestations of Indian religious art to mere objects of cult. The very plasticity inherent in them must be recognised as evidence of their discreteness and autonomy. The rhythm that beats through them is the rhythm of the individual creative temperament and not of a collective entity. The forms of Indian art, in common with those of all other arts, are the result of personal divinations, inventiveness and unforeseen revelations, and not the translation of yogic attitudes and of a specific religious symbolism. As in all other lands, the symbols and attributes are merely decorative marginal notes on the main coherent linear statement presented to our judgement.

In criticising the tendencies with which I have been dealing, I hope I have indicated to some extent the method I would like to see adopted for the study of the history of our fine arts. If I have belittled the methods that have prevailed till now, it is because each of them has claimed, consciously or unconsciously, to be the only one for the interpretation of our art. I have attacked the irrelevancy of the first, the frivolity of the second and the inadequacy of the third school. In advocating a more comprehensive approach I would not eschew some of the elements from these methods, if the first two might be dignified by that name. I would like to include in it the enthusiasm of the nationalists, for without fervour all subjects of study are lifeless; within well-defined limits I would accept the subjectivism of the aesthetes, for the sincere apprehension of beauty is an incentive in our pursuit. But these are merely pragmatic concessions. I have greater respect for the writers of the third school for they at least have knowledge. They attempt to dive into the secrets of the creative process in the mind of the artist, though to me they remain hopelessly unaware of the unrepeatability of his exacting personality. They wrongly identify the inspiration with the inspired. I regard art also as a related phenomenon, only one aspect of our cultural life. But I maintain that it has an identity and integrity of its own. Our attempt should be to investigate its distinct being, standing out independently from other sociological phenomena and yet at the same time situated amongst them. The main pre-occupation of the history of art should be the study of the development of form and the evolution of technique which has made that form realisable. Both these depend on the growth of our material civilization and our political history. We have to follow up, through the ages, the ever-increasing power of man over his material but we must hear in mind that the development of art rarely coincides with the chronology of history. Styles, designs, patterns, tricks of composition, use of colour achieve perfection, as other cultural phenomena also do, by sometimes reverting to their origin. To trace thus the life of an art object and the different stages which have contributed to its final shape, it is necessary to have a wide knowledge of the vagaries of form in other cultures. Moreover, it is a rare thing for an artist, in a moment of inspiration, to bring to life an entirely original form. Like most things it is influenced either by tradition, which has integrated it as the only adequate expression of a specific sensibility, or else by contact with the products of foreign cultures. Most art objects in India are composite of these indigenous or foreign influences. A work of art of our middle ages often is an epitome of age-long conflicts and harmonies among combating racial propensities as well as between indigenous and imported taste. The method I recommend may by called sociological. It is not new, only recent. It has the sanction of the most important treatises on the history of art today. It has the advantage of removing distinctions between the history of art in different lands by generalising the principles which condition the life of art everywhere. It studies the current taste, the political circumstances, the social background, the philosophical trend of thought of a period in order to elucidate those factors which confine an artist's mind but which can never dominate or suppress his creative urge. Among these limiting factors this method gives a place of importance to race and foreign cultural contacts. It is now an admitted fact that in spite of migrations, changes in modes of living and political fortunes, racial tastes and skill always persist. They are only repressed for a while. Blood seems to have a deeper memory than the human mind and sometimes even symbols of long-forgotten beliefs make an unexpected appearance. Influences of foreign cultures, whether accepted voluntarily or because of political exigencies, also survive. Acquired methods of overpowering the resistance of material are rarely permitted to lapse when they spell economy, rapidity and ease. Sometimes the same alien influence may dominate, as Hellenism did in Gandhara, or become transfigured in a national synthesis as under the T'ang in China, but in both cases, conquering or vanquished, it constitutes a part of succeeding history. Not only is its actual contribution to form or technique unquestionable but we must take account of it even when we characterise it as non-valid, because it is in the struggle against it that new forms come into being. Nothing is taken away from the prestige of any art to acknowledge its debt to foreign influences. Some cultural milieus are so vital that they absorb and transform them or force them to their needs. Classical India, China and Byzantium, to name only three cultural groups, succeeded in assimilating the outer influences to the exigencies of their aesthetic demand. This method also maintains that form in art is not indissolubly connected with its content but with its technique. We recognise the validity of this in our own time because of the abstraction in visualising matter which is employed by the cubists and their extreme groups, the suprematists and the dadaists. It is the study of technique, the valiant conquest of the human race over dead material, which is most lacking in the history of Indian art. It is not religious subjects, nor the wealth of our artistic imaginativeness, which distinguishes our art from that of others but its unequalled virtuosity in technique. Whether in sculpture or in the industrial arts, no material, stone or metal or wood, has been able to resist subservience to our most extravagant phantasy. We have combined different metals, we have united stone with metal and stone with stone as no other people in the world has been able to do, and we have possessed a technical mastery which has made us envisage unterrified any subject, however incompatible it be with our empirical existence.

I advocate this method with a purpose. Before concluding I shall touch very briefly on an application of it which I commend to your attention. You must have heard that in recent times some western scholars have been deeply engaged in discovering the influence of nomads, chiefly Iranians, on the art of their countries. Forty-five years ago Kondakov established the import of Iranian elements into Byzantine art. Russian scholars, who were his followers, accepted Iranism because they found that the Hellenistic theory could not explain away the difficult problems besetting the origin and forms of Scythian art. Since the chance find of the Oxus Treasure and the Sassanian silver platters, researches in Celtic art and the art of the Great Migration, excavations in Mesopotamia, Asia Minor and Crete, the discovery of the art of Central Asia and Luristan, investigations in early Chinese art and in Japanese art of the Nara period, since the Turki and Mongolian finds, we have come into possession of a new clue which we hope will ultimately elucidate the interchange of art forms in Asia and Europe. The Persian Exhibition of London in 1931 brought to a focus researches in this direction. The dynastic art of Iran and Asiatic miniature painting, to mention only two subjects, have recently been studied from this point of view. The greatest attention is being paid to the chalcolithic period and to the Iranian migration in proto-history. There are brilliant scholars and art historians who have taken up this work. Among them I might mention Rostovtseff in America, Strzygowski in Austria, Tallgren in Finland, Minns and Dalton in England, Takacsz and Fettich in Hungary, Andersen in Sweden, Millet in France, Sarre and Herzfeld in Germany and Katakami in Japan. In Prague, scholars belonging to the Russian emigration have founded the Institut Kondakovianum, named after the great byzantologist, which under the direction of Kalitinsky, has been publishing a marvellous periodical specially devoted to the study of the nomads and the distribution by them of specific art motifs and compositional arrangements. This is a fascinating subject and should surely be studied with reference to our own art. I may mention here that when, during the International Congress of the History of Art at Stockholm in 1933, I had sketched the possibilities of this study, it was received with a great deal of interest by the Iranists assembled there. It is true that because of India's geographical position she could not serve as a great centre for the interchange of art forms, such as the steppe zone from Korea to the Carpathians did. Racial infiltration in our country, after the Aryan migration, was also rarely of a mass character. The foreign nomadic dynasties that came to India had already had a period of settled existence and retained a dim memory of their previous mode of living. Moreover, they adopted India as their home and from the outset had to contend against a vital indigenous culture. But still we cannot ignore the fact that, during long centuries, we were ruled by the Kushan branch of the Iranian nomadic tribe of the Yuë-chis, and it was under them that many beginnings were made in Indian art. We cannot but be struck in Kushan sculpture by an uncanny observation, a marvellous sense of modelling, a poise and an accretion of traits and symbols hearkening back to a non-Indian past. The domination of Western India by the Sakas and later of Central India by the White Huns, also Iranian nomads, have left vestiges in our art forms which it would be well worth our while to trace. Most examples of our classical art are reflections of court culture, so it is to the industrial arts, especially to folk art, that we have to turn to disengage the Iranian element. I am convinced that the pursuit of this enquiry will prove fruitful and be of immense importance to our art history. It will destroy, among other things, the narrowness of the generally accepted conception of our art.

I therefore suggest that for the future study of our subject the sociological method offers a greater scope. The modern investigator, alive to the importance of race, influences, root forms, traditions, the history of technique, etc., must maintain the disparateness of art from other sociological phenomena and yet be aware of its dependence of them. Whilst recognising the collective pressure, he must insist on the inviolability of the freedom of the individual creative spirit. It is essential for him to possess a catholicity of taste and wide aesthetic sympathies, the diversity of art manifestations meaning nothing more to him than chance specific applications of certain fundamental principles governing creation in all cultures. Thus he should be capable of reacting as sensitively to the Greek ideal of the deified man as to the Indian ideal of the humanised divinity.

2

Art and Education*

Out of the various subjects proposed to me for this evening's address, some of which would have been more attractive for you and easier for me to discourse upon, I have deliberately chosen the connection between Art (a word I shall use in the sense of the fine arts) and Education because of its importance in the scheme of cultural reconstruction which must be the ultimate aim of all national education. I welcome this opportunity of being able to present before you teachers, who have gathered in such large numbers from all parts of Bengal and who have the power to exercise your influence for good or for evil on tender sensibilities, a point of view which unfortunately is often neglected when we come to appraise the true ends of education.

To begin with, let us be franks and admit that, whatever voices be raised in the wilderness, all real interest in India today is concentrated solely in the political struggle. The best brains of the country, all the passion, temperament and energy, all the capacity for intransigence or accommodation are engaged in trying to rear up the scaffolding of a political edifice. In the zest of that struggle, in the bickerings and injustices of political life, our leaders for the most part are utterly unmindful of the form and design with which such a building shall ultimately be invested. Is it to be European, its facade subjected to the rhythm of fenestration, an efficient, sanitary, ultra-modern spacious habitation, or is it to be a palace like Man Singh's at Gwalior,

---

* Delivered at the Conference of the Secondary Teachers of Bengal during the Bengal Education Week, 1936.

cool, semi-subterranean, with painted lintels and carved columns, a place for contemplative repose and luxury after the heaviness of wars, or shall it be arched, turretted, firmly planted on the earth, solid on thick stone plinths, like the vigorous, defiant palace-fortresses of the Pathans at Mandou? Dispassionately watching events, I am afraid it is more likely to be, as most of our public and private buildings are today, a hybrid structure with Gothic openings, French mansards, Moorish pilasters stuck into Roman vaults, Hindu pavilions stretching over Ionic pillars, a faithful reflection of our minds, tawdry, incoherent and joyless. If such is the indifference of our political workers to the architectural unity of the edifice they desire to construct, how can one wonder that they have little thought for the other than material life of those who will occupy it in the future? I realise there is a time in the life of every country when the creative energy is inevitably devoted to political re-adjustments. May be, ours is going through this phase and there are reasons, historical and economic, which might explain our obsession. But the claims of culture are equally urgent and have been regarded as such during the bitterest period of political struggle in those countries which usually are held up to us for our ideal. To those who are deep sighted, or who, like you and me, are out of the mêlée and have some time for reflection, the activity, now prevailing in India, amounts to the fabrication of a frame, to borrow an analogy from my subject, without thought of the picture which it is going to enclose. It is therefore essential for us to have an accurate and correct estimate of our national cultural assets, a true apprehension of our originality and our contributive value to the world, before we definitely fix on the form which our political strivings should take. I am convinced that the most ardent of our westernisers will admit that political freedom is not worthy of attainment, if a country, like India, which for so long has been as emporium of ideas, style, colour and inventions in art technique, should be one among many in which drabness is inseparable from the achievements of democracy. We must therefore strongly condemn our nationalists who lost the miraculous opportunity for the resuscitation of Indian design offered to them by the partial successful revival of our textile handicraft due to *swadeshi* and allowed the movement to degenerate into a competition for possessing the Indian market with imitations of cheap European models. Their action would have been more in consonance with the pathos of their declared faith, had they encouraged our traditional taste, which has been for centuries the envy of the discerning and the sensitive in western countries.

At the present moment, owing to unfortunate economic conditions, the education that is generally advocated by those in authority is of a narrow utilitarian scope. It is possible that for a short transitory period and under the compulsion of unusual circumstances this is the kind of education which is needed by the province and the country. But the ends of education properly understood are surely other than to befit a person solely for a lucrative vocation. Even in a strictly utilitarian conception of education, it might cogently be argued that the equipment needed for a successful vocational career should necessarily include a knowledge of those external factors, which condition one's labour, and which relate it to the outer world. We know from experience that a background of culture, the habit of reflectiveness, adaptability and the faculty of critically revaluing tradition, have always distinguished the good craftsman from the bad. Hence, if we believe with Plato that education does not consist in a process of acquisition but in the development of powers already existing in us, we shall find that nothing is useless which helps to broaden our vision and encourage our sympathies. The artistic instinct in us is one of those latent forces to which Plato refers. From our childhood, by the slow process of recognition and differentiation, our vision gets acquainted with the particularity of forms, and the next stage in our development logically leads us to a compelling necessity to exteriorise our impressions of the outer world with the help of symbols and signs. As we grow older, we strive to achieve the maximum of completeness available to us in interpretation and thus it happens that very early we attempt graphic or sonorous descriptions of things we have seen or felt. This urge for giving form to the accumulation of our observations of the life around us is also noticeable in the case of the primitive man, whose first gratuitous activity consisted in perfecting the shape of his tools and in inscribing on the walls of caves, with a rare avoidance of rhetoric which so often mars the art of later days, his pictorial impressions of animal movements. The faculty of sensing visual relatedness in the midst of the divergent phenomena of life and this early striving after mastery over matter which, when it attains to realisation, we call technique, lie at the base of the artistic creative urge. As we advance in years, or, as the early unions of man develop into complex entities, the vividness and immediacy of our reaction to the outer world ceases and the forms that we find in use around us impinge upon our minds. It is in this way that tradition grows; for the individual abdicates his vision to the community. Having admitted that exteriorisation in forms is an inherent necessity in man we may go a step further and maintain that from our earliest years we experience a pleasurable reaction to pleasant forms and colours, which themselves may be termed uncontoured forms in space. This to begin with is individual, but it is a curious fact, as we grow up, we often find that the race or tribe in which we are born has also had similar reactions and has tried to express them in a manner akin to our own. In milieus, where tradition is a living influence, we grow gradually accustomed to take pleasure in these forms as they adequately answer to our need for integrity of texture, rhythm, proportion or phantasy. These needs differ with different races and countries, and therefore the art forms of one country do not necessarily stand superior to those of another, for the only distinguishing feature, which enables us to establish a hierarchy among the achievements of art in different centres, is the continued presence of freshness of inspiration, vividness of representation and inventiveness in execution. No other criterion rules aesthetic judgment. If you believe with me that the apprehension of Beauty is a source of pleasure (I use the word in its Aristotelian sense of rational enjoyment), that its contemplation gives us an insight into the Ideal Form, that it enriches our spirit and helps us to discriminate between evil and good, as the ancients held, that it develops in us the sense of tact and balance, you must admit that the results we obtain are the same as those at which all true education aims. Tomorrow from this very place you will hear my friend, Professor Satyen Bose, the brilliant Indian scientist, tell you of the supreme value his subject has for education. I do not dispute his claim, but I hold that the development of the human spirit, and the joy which is the ultimate goal of our mental strivings, is not exclusively distilled from any one branch of knowledge. The quest of beauty is as much a search after truth as the pursuit of her by the scientist or the philosopher. I hear it too often contended that a man might be educated and cultured and yet not be responsive to beauty. This can only mean that he does not derive satisfaction from outward forms but from the cogency of intellectual systems, whether of philosophy, law, or science. But the need remains the same, the need for symmetry, balance and coherence. If it were possible to give visual or audible forms to these systems of thought or experience, they would evoke appreciation in the same way as music, architecture, painting or sculpture. In fact, it is impossible for men as normal beings to escape in any of their activities, which aim at perfection, from a feeling which, though not identical with, is akin to aesthetic satisfaction.

Having discussed so for the connection between Art and Education, a fact now accepted by educationists in Scandinavia, Czechoslovakia, Japan and the United States of America, to name but a few countries which I have deliberately chosen because of the large diffusion in them of technical vocational training, I regret to say that in our present system of education the teaching of art occupies an almost non-existent place. It is roughly ten years ago that the late Sir Asutosh Mookerjee introduced the subject of fine arts in the curriculum of our University's post-graduate studies. The students that come to us have no initial preparation and, for the first year, are wholly at a loss to orientate themselves in the midst of examples that illustrate the many-sidedness of ancient Indian artistic achievement. Some years ago a scheme beginning at the matriculation stage for graded acquaintance with the masterpieces of our own art, as well as with those of other nations, was suggested to the University, but so far no steps have been taken to put it into execution. We must confess that the passionate advocacy by Coomaraswamy and others, Indian and European, for a place for art in national life has miserably failed in our province. It is true that in your schools you teach drawing, clay modelling and fancy needlework. But these are mere rudiments and only in their developed state of picture, sculpture, decorative design, might be called art. Moreover, your aim in teaching these subjects is neither to stimulate artistic creation, nor to prepare your pupils for a craftsman's vocation, but merely to help to concentrate their attention during class hours and to develop dexterity of fingers. Dexterity alone is a far prelude to skill and has only a disciplinary value.

You will ask me then, given the present state of things, with little hope of change in the near future, what is one to do with the teaching of fine arts in the schools. I am conscious of the difficulties. I realise that art will never occupy the place in our society as it did in the past of our country, unless a complete change occurs in our mental and moral outlook. The task is colossal. We have to transform our entire surroundings, to get rid of the ugliness with which we encumber our houses and persons, to free our brains and hearts from both the disparagement and the undue adulation of our cultural heritage, to train the mind to detect achievement in terms of the creative intention, and specially to cultivate a sympathy with forms that at first sight appear unusual. I know the sense of discomfort that one experiences in the presence of unusual forms; how the eye is more conservative than any other part of the human organism and what a slow process is needed to disengage the elements of beauty in objects which testify to an unwonted phantasy. But if one is patient and humble, as one must be before manifestations of human temperament and talent, if one is successful in penetrating to the secrets of the mind that creates a given image, the image will live and illumine one's spirit. The attitude of piety I suggest is necessary for the understanding of every art and especially of our own, for we are in a state of moral confusion far worse than any other people. We are neither orientals nor westerners. We have been taught western literature and our minds have been filled with western imagery. Our education has had a background of a foreign landscape. The result is that we have no comprehension of either western or eastern forms. The blight of bad taste has fallen upon the representations of the gods and goddesses themselves that are worshipped. The sources of Indian art have completely dried. The grand tradition of our medieval sculpture, which knew how to inform stone with miraculous movements in order to portray the lives of gods involved in human relations, that splendid realisation of the Indian ideal of god-man, unparalleled in the world's art for plasticity and dramatism, has been allowed to lapse into oblivion. We are equally ignorant of the masterpieces of western art. We do not know the compassionate tenderness of Early Christian icons, the pageant of Byzantine mosaic, we have not even heard the names of those magicians of the Renaissance, of Bellini, Mantegna, Simone di Martini, Piero della Francesca. Art study and art appreciation is banished from our lives. We not only surround ourselves with ugliness but are proud of it. We even consider it to be a help in the intellectual and spiritual development which is claimed to be peculiarly ours. In our society today the slovenly, the unkempt and the unseemly is held up not only as an object of admiration but of emulation.

Of course you cannot help all this. Your school houses may sometimes be practical but they have been built by the Public Works Department, and I know in what relation they stand to beauty. And this has occurred in a province where folk taste manifests itself in the most exquisite of lines in the humblest of dwellings. Your economic position is such that neither you nor your students can travel and get acquainted at first hand with the monuments of our art. Your libraries, if you have any, are not provided with books, for the most part expensive, which contain illustrations of art objects. Your knowledge of what has been achieved in the past, and is being attempted now, is necessarily based on cheap unconscientious reprints which appear in the so-called progressive press. Even if some of you are endowed with artistic sensibility and interest, you cannot help your pupils because they come to you, with their visions already distorted in the primary schools. The situation is really hopeless and no remedy will avail unless a courageous remodelling of our educational policy, involving the lowest stages of instruction, will enable every important branch of your national culture to find its rightful place in the curriculum of studies.

Even in the educational organization, such as it exists today, I would like to suggest to you two ways in which you could encourage acquaintance with art and aid to develop the artistic aptitude of those who are under your charge. The first would be to treat art as a helpmate of history; the second, to assist directly in the conservation of whatever remains of Indian art traditions from disappearance in your own towns and villages. I shall treat both these subjects separately.

Until recently, since the discovery of Indian art and the movement for its preservation, Indian history, especially of the ancient period, was but a dry narrative of political events. Art objects not only illustrate cultural contrasts and fusions, the conflicts of influences, the stories of racial supremacy, but reveal changes and evolution in taste due to newer spiritual and material demands. They visually illumine and correlate the facts of history and make them alive. How much better do we understand the story of the mission of faith sent by Asoka to Antioch and Egypt, when we regard the monumental examples of the art of that period deriving its traditions from the Great King of Kings, whose satrapy, till late, much of the Buddhist kingdom was. Whatever one might think of the theory of the importation of Iranian workmen into Pataliputra, one cannot fail to see in the vast Mauryan Empire, with its cultural prestige and military prowess, a conscious resurrection of the glorious traditions of the Achaemenians destroyed by Alexander. In the elegant terracottas left by the Sungas, replete with delicacy of execution and a certain languorous tastefulness, we see the luxury and decadence of court life during a period of comparative tranquillity, while the Bharhut stupa shows us the wealth and prosperity and the naïve personal vanity of the middle classes of those days, paying to get their portraits sculptured in awkward devotional poses. In the art of the Kushans you easily detect the throbbing life of the time, their continental orientation, the foreign racial taste reminiscent of the days of exile before they reached Bactria, the fine modelling and quick observation of a youthful, vital, energetic people, who not so long ago were nomads. What can better illustrate the organic fusion under one supreme sway of conflicting racial contributions, the splendour and the wisdom of the Imperial Guptas, their humanism, their solid international and colonial status than the examples of our classical sculpture? How can one share in the religious ecstasy of our Middle Ages without Ellora? Coming down to a much later period, in Mughal painting we see the evolution of those hardy fighters of Central Asia, descendants of Chenghiz and Timur, transformed by Indian conditions and Persian influence, unmindful of nomadic tents and traits of tribal life which so largely figure in their earlier works, becoming the most magnificent of India Emperors and vying with the Safavids to establish their claim to be the only worthy successors in the East of the brilliant Sassanian monarchy. And in Rajput paintings, is there not the sheltered, idyllic life of a proud-hearted people nurtured in Vaishnavite lyricism, penned in the outward pressure, but gathering strength in silence and isolation for the final assault? One could go on enumerating instances, and it is for you to take advantage of art objects to reconstitute Indian history, to bring out its truth and to dispel with their aid much that has accumulated of bias and unreliable interpretation.

The second way you could help the propagation of art study is by conscientiously trying to revive our decaying handicrafts.

Those of you who come from the countryside, and especially those who are teachers in village schools, have the chance of being in touch with local productions. I hope you have under your charge a number of pupils who will not come to this town for university degrees and swell the company of the unemployed, but will be content to turn their energies to more profitable occupations. Before advising a pupil to take up a vocational career it is always better to choose one who has hereditary advantages in that direction. Once you know his decision, it should be your duty to get him acquainted with indigenous patterns and colours and to encourage in him all efforts at originality but after you have carefully grounded him in the tendencies of local needs. I do not think that, where handicrafts still live, there is a risk of your pupil turning out completely new designs which will have no commercial value; he would rather content himself with variations on accepted motifs; for, once a child's eye has been trained to beauty and rhythm, he is not likely to diverge from a satisfying standard. But the difficulty is that in most localities, through want of patronage, handicrafts have been allowed to die. In other countries of the world, schoolmasters have proved most helpful in resuscitating them by propagandizing their consumption in preference to machine-made objects where utility and cheapness, more often than not, destroy the elements of beauty. I shall not tire you by citing the ethical and cultural advantages of handicraft over machine-made articles. A little thinking on your part will convince you that, apart from the intrinsic merit of the personal touch, even for articles made on the mould, the conditions under which handicraft is produced are more humane, healthy and moral. A village school might serve as a nucleus for local handicraft products and, by exchanges and loans, enrich its collections. I am on principle not much in favour of museums, even school museums, for it is better that these articles should be in constant use in the home and not lie relegated to cupboards. But at a time when the arts are becoming extinct, there is no other way left but to save them by collecting them in museums. It is indeed sad that one should have to suggest these directions to an audience belonging to a province the folk art of which is the backbone of its culture and which can rival with any in grace and vitality.

Before I conclude, I shall ask your permission to digress and take the liberty of warning you against a common danger in the teaching of art. The training of the art sensibility of a child is an extremely delicate matter. Whatever else one does, one should not make one's pupils conscious of artiness, of a deliberate intention to produce beautiful effects. In art, as in religion, the best is always he who is not constantly mindful of meritorious deeds. Otherwise, you are bound to inculcate priggishness in your work and in art criticism there is hardly a more blameworthy characterisation. I would not like our handicraft to take on the colour of a revival such as that of the William Morris cult in England which has degenerated into snobbish products made in the workshops of Chelsea and Chipping Campden for the arty middle-class. We should be warned by the fate of an intentional revival nearer home, by the example of the Bengali School of Painting where, with the exception of a few outstanding creative talents, there is a straining after prettiness and the picturesque so utterly at variance with the bold, unassuming painting of our classical and folk art.

You, the teachers of Bengal, are best fitted to instil reverence and love into the minds of the young for our artistic past and for a future organically connected with that past and yet responsive to newer demands. But you yourselves must first believe that, from amongst our heritage, the artistic, embodying as it does in concrete and comparatively imperishable form the passionate longings and the spiritual realisations of you country, is the one that is likely to live longest in the world's memory. I would wish you to subscribe to this article of faith, that our ancient art has been one of the most adequate vehicles for the expression of the inner life of man, and deservedly holds the position of honour which it does today amongst the arts of the other countries. If you are convinced of the utility of art in education and of their intimate connection with national culture, you yourselves, by study and observation, must be the first to be trained to appreciation and appraisement, lest you become like the guardians of whom Plato speaks 'who, by being educated in the midst of ill-representations, might contract imperceptibly some mighty evil in their souls.'

3

Introduction to Indo-Persian Painting

I

It might appear strange to some of you that I have chosen for the title of my lecture the obsolete term Indo-Persian, which has been rejected by almost all the historians of Indian art. The principal objection to it is due to the fact that its use might suggest that Mughal art was nothing more than merely a reflection of Indian and Persian art traditions, having no discrete existence of its own. Whilst in its maturer periods Mughal art did possess an individuality and formed by itself an organised unit, it is no slur on its later phases if we characterise its beginnings and the persistent direction of its revivalist inclinations as a striving after the transference of Persian conventions to an Indian setting. At its very outset, however, before the Persian and Indian elements had been organically transfused, it has a specific artistic flavour of its own comparable to that of the verses of Amir Khusru before the emergence of Urdu. This early period is often described as a servile imitation of Persian models, but it appears as wrong to assert this as to say that there was nothing individual in the writings of those Indian poets who used the Persian language as their medium of expression. It is true that, compared to the brilliant achievements of Herat and even Ispahan, some of these early works do present schematic colour, relations and a deplorable looseness of composition such as many centuries ago, the Hellenistic art of Gandhara did in contrast to the monuments of Greece and Asia Minor; but, as in the later case, there are exceptions, notable not only for their intrinsic worth but as points of radiation of artistic influence. The works produced under Humayun and Akbar may be termed a colonial expression of Persian art, with all the implications of transformation and adaptability which the word 'colonial' connotes in culture and literature. Whatever may be their value to the aesthete—and surely some remarkable things were created at this epoch, for example, the brilliantly composed pictures dealing with Firoz Shah, the King of Bengal, one of which is perhaps the best representative, outside Herat, of the school of Bihzad,—to an art historian these early works are an important store-house of knowledge from which may be disengaged in later products those formative elements which constitute their pictorial foundation.

There are some writers who concede the employment of the term 'Indo-Persian' to the work done under the first two Mughal emperors but object to extending it to later periods. This seems illogical, for, if its use evokes in our mind the most important constituent currents of this art, there is no reason why it may not be employed to cover the entire period of its existence. We all know that, even after Mughal art had reached its culminating point and had become an integral part of Indian culture, there were painters under Shahjehan and later, who, tired of portraiture or *genre* painting in the new style, were either copying or doing original work in the Irani *qalam*. As a matter of fact the Irani *qalam* is persistent up to the present day and its unique appeal will die only when Persia ceases to live and influence. But one may go farther in the use of the term 'Indo-Persian,' even though this might appear most heterodox, and include, because of reasons which will be given later, many works executed with another intention, the Hindu or the Rajput, so called at times justifiably for the sake of ease in classification but more often with a desire to assert their utter independence of the main stream of Indian art, which, during the xvi and xvii centuries, happened to be flowing at Agra, Delhi and Aurangabad under non-Indian and non-Hindu rulers. This, the central idea of my address, should be made quite clear at the outset. We are all aware of the distinction—and many of them are of a deep nature—which exist between what are termed Mughal and Rajput art. There are some outstanding differences which will be dealt with later, but it should be remembered that it is impossible to study these arts without recognising their close interdependence and the contribution of one to the growth of the other, and without constant reference to the two traditions which constitute their source. They are both expressions of a creative impulse made possible by the splendour and organisation of the Indo-Persian princes, the chief difference between the two being that one drew its subjects more from Indian religious lore and the other more from the profane urbanity of Persian ways.

In order to make this point clear a digression may be permitted and facts, though well-known, may be repeated so that the problem can be seen in its true perspective. The great name in the history of painting in Persia, as well as in India, during the xvi century is Bihzad. The work of this gifted artist at Herat and of his followers was a constant model to Mughal painters, though Persia had produced some of its most exquisite painting just before him and Bihzad, with an extraordinary genius for artistic combination, had contrived to unite the traditional elements into an eclectic whole. He was no innovator but a conservative creator with an inspired eye for pleasurable selection and arrangement. The name of the Raphael of the East given to him by some writers on Persian art seems particularly inept, for Raphael's pictures are characterised by an astounding factura which is not always present in Bihzad's work; but the Persian painter resembles that great Renaissance master because the work of both, though derivative, is grounded on a purely pictorial synthesis. No extraneous feeling, religious or profane, excites them; they revel in the pure joy of painting, in the marvel of line and colour for the sake of the painting itself. To be better than Bihzad or even to be his equal was the highest praise that could be lavished on an artist. It is for this reason that Abul Fazl, in a mood of exaggerated and unconscientious flattery, maintains the superiority of his master's artists over this wizard of Persian painting.

Like most orientals the Persians did not possess a great interest in perspective. Their pictures were book illustrations and were meant to be looked at from above and not in a diagonal or in a straight line from the eye as in western paintings. One should not, however, suppose that the Persians were incapable of perspective drawing. You have only to see some of their best-known pictures to notice how the masses on the sky line are arranged in diminution, and where not deliberately distorted for pictorial effect, the third plane is in scientific perspective. Generally the figures and elements in the first two planes are of equal size; sometimes those in the first plane, if unimportant for the action, are smaller than those in the second. This shows that scientific perspective though understood and often employed, was not considered an absolutely necessary constituent of every picture as demanded by western tradition today. The chief aim of the Persian artist was centrality; as long as the attention was effectively focussed on the centre of the picture, it did not matter if the eye roamed to either end and found on both sides the pictorial elements in diminution. From this importance given to centrality one can easily deduce the inevitable passage of Persian art, and of its closest follower, that of the Mughals, towards portraiture. Persian art is also the art of the line and not of volume. In this direction it attained a virtuosity and inventiveness unrivalled by any art of the middle ages, not even the Chinese, to which it owes so much for its technique and early inspiration. Both Mughal and Rajput art are also exclusively founded on the line, a tradition which we might call Asiatic, for we find the line to be the basis of the best frescoes at Ajanta and elsewhere, such as in Tuen Huang in Eastern Turkestan or at Horuyuji in Japan, where the original impulse came from India. The centrality of action refers only to the aesthetic action of the eye in encompassing the picture. It does not allude to a deliberate intention on the part of the Persian painters to limit our awareness to dramatic events taking place in the centre of the picture. In fact, of all the arts, Persian painting is least concerned with dramatic feeling. This must be a survival of early Byzantine influence, noticeable also in the art products of the Sassanians. This particular trait forms one of the most important distinctions between the art of the Persians and that of the Arabs, who, from the beginning of pictorial art among them, have awkwardly and often incapably struggled to depict semitic anthropocentric sentiments. To a careless observer, however, Persian art may also suggest the dramatic because its compositional arrangements often deal with animated scenes peopled with human figures and an atmosphere of animation not infrequently engenders a sense of the drama. But this is illusory and accidental. Nothing could be farther from the Persian artist's intention. In is best creations he is utterly devoid of that intense striving, so characteristic of the Indian tradition, to solve his pictorial problem with the help of formal contrasts. Mughal pictures in their formative and classical stages tried to adopt, though with little success, the Persian manner, but they could not withstand the pressure of contemporary Hindu painting, which was replete with movement and action, often tending in the works of some of the lesser known schools even towards theatricality.

The aim of the Persian painter thus was to establish beauty by the arrangement of the pictorial elements at his disposal with the deliberate intention of producing artistic effect. Being impervious to all emotions except the search after beauty, his creations, in their subtle mingling of bright colours and fluent line, had alliances with glowing mosaics or lovely carpets. He opens up to one a world where both the painter and the spectator delight in the beauty of flowers, in the gold, white, deep red and bright blue with which their world is bathed, in coral shaped mountains, curling *tai* clouds, blossoming trees, fleet-limbed animals, gorgeous dresses. His vision is of paradise, a word with Achaemenian associations, where all is exquisiteness of form and purity of colour. Neither the Mughal nor the Rajput, the one with his masterly draughtsmanship and the other with his luminous colours, except in rare instances, attained the joyous beauty of Persian painting in which the delight of the painter in the subject was such that his design often overflowed the bands of flowery diapers which usually encompass his pictures. The striving after a deliberate pictorial effect is an inheritance which, with varying success, persisted throughout the range of Mughal painting. It is not that the Hindus absolutely rejected this principle; though perhaps reluctantly they did make use of it during the period of the full blossoming of their art, the only thing that may be maintained is that the purely pictorial intention, as distinct from the dramatic, is foreign and generally distasteful to Indian tradition and temperament.

Some of the original features of Persian painting have been briefly indicated in order that attention may be directed to those elements which derived from that source in Indian mediaeval art. In the earlier works of the Mughals one is presented with the same seemingly haphazard disposition of pictorial elements, a similar discursiveness, but without that inner pictorial cohesion and compositional unity which characterised Bihzad and his immediate precursors. The colours, though as costly and recherché as in Persia, to the preparation of which, according to Abul Fazl, his Royal Master gave his personal attention, do not possess the same lustre and enamel-like quality, though, strangely enough, this is often to be found among the Rajputs. The Persian conventions of the high ridge against the sky line, of filling one side of the picture with architecture, of the central carpet, not in relief but as a rectangular design in colour with seated figures, the coral hills ending in animal heads, a survival of Iranian nomadic tradition, the laying of scenes in ravines between two mountains, all these are adopted but usually incapably utilised. A compositional convention of particular interest to us is the one in which the main action is preceded by a foreground of crenelated architectural fences usually with a stream flowing below, carrying birds and flowers. This setting Strzygowski has claimed to be an essential element in what he calls *hvarena* landscape, originating from Nordic Iranian experience; it is a landscape bathed in the glow of holiness which emanates from Ahura Mazda. He has pointed out its presence at Ajanta and in the beautiful Byzantine mosaics of Ravenna. This convention is to be found in a large number of Mughal and Rajput work, but has never been so extensively or appropriately employed as in the Deccan, in centres geographically close to Ajanta, at Aurangabad, Golconda and Bijapur. Coming back to early Mughal art, the absence of those supreme factors present in every good Persian work, namely, quality and finish, is most noticeable. These have been Iran's contribution to Asiatic art from classical times, as students of Mauryan and Kushan art in India will have observed. But the Mughal painters even at this early stage show remarkable gift for drawing, and one can already discern how eventually they will surpass their masters in draughtsmanship. They are keener observers of realistic plasticity than the Persians, but, in these early pictures, except when the composition is small, they fail to give full effect to their gift because of incompetent spacing and a lack of feeling for air. The Persians, too, have examples of firm and realistic drawing, but it is something of a side line. There are two pictures on the walls of the Chehel Sutun at Ispahan, done under the Safavids, one of which represents Shah Tahmasp entertaining Humayun, a fugitive at his court, with wine, and dancing, where the drawing, tactfully controlled, is of great fineness. But even this cannot compare with the best work of the school of Jehangir, such as the portrait of Ala-al-mulk Tuni by Chitarman, evidently executed with the famous one-haired brush of the Mughal painters, or the head of Akbar in the India Office Library. In this connection I would like you to notice the happy grouping and masterly drawing of a number of Hindu Saints which forms part of a larger picture called 'The Dance of Dervishes' in the possession of Captain Spencer-Churchill, reproduced, because of its outstanding quality, as a separate plate in that delightful book *The Court Painters of the Mughals*. There is no doubt in my mind that the art of perfect draughtsmanship is a part of the Indian heritage, for not only in Ajanta, at a particular phase, was all attention devoted to precision and finish of contours but the exactitude of line and controlled firmness of hand is also an outstanding feature of the Jaina miniatures as well as of the best examples of the Jaipur *qalam*.

The Mughals borrowed from the Persians not merely the technique but also the subject matter of their pictures. Roughly catalogued, the subjects they dealt with were battle scenes, animals and birds, scenes of hunting, gardens and palaces during construction showing the remarkable building energy of the emperors, discussion among divines and, especially portraiture. Except for a few attempts, Mughal art did not concern itself with the illustration of narrative poems or epic an literary romantic episodes, but in most examples it wound itself round the personality of the rulers who patronised it. As these sovereigns were constantly engaged in conquest, early Mughal painting deals largely with battles, models for which were ready to hand in the Persian illustrations to the Shah-nameh. In Mughal art we find in large numbers drawings of animals and birds, often with a semi-scientific end. This is an ancient Islamic practices, which provided an outlet for the representational instinct so ruthlessly limited by religious usage, as can be seen in Arab manuscripts of the so-called Mesopotamian school of the xiii century under the Abbasids. Mountains, called coral, are also of Arab origin and are an important decorative feature in a large number of Persian, Mughal and Rajput pictures. For some indefinable reason their conventional form and texture were connected in the minds of the Arabs with the mountains of India, and in Persian painting too these became necessary elements for producing an exotic atmosphere.

Scenes of the chase, specially connected with the legend of Bahram Gor, fill the pages of Persian books. These are traceable to an earlier period of Iranian art, to the Sassanians, who depicted them on their silver platters and silken stuffs. The Mughal and the Rajput have made large use of the theme to the glory of their rulers, who were passionate huntsmen, and also because such scenes afford remarkable opportunities for plastic drawing and elaborate compositional arrangements. The swift-limbed and gentle eyed antelope, the symbol of goodness, is favourite motif with both Mughal and Rajput painters and is hardly ever absent from pictures depicting the hunt.

Conversation among divines in a garden is also a frequent Persian theme, especially at Herat. These take place in an atmosphere of great peace and reasonableness, except for one well-known scene from the time of Tahmasp,—that vainglorious prince who can compare with a modern cinema star in the quantity of portraits painted of him in different postures and situations—where one divine, or probably he is a physician, knocks down the other in the presence of the enthroned monarch. There are several pictures dealing with this theme ascribed to Bihzad, and though they are very ingenious and colourful as all his work is, they do not exhibit the same quiet and charm which we find in the best Mughal interpretations, where the psychological situation is exploited to the utmost. Treated with sobriety and decorum this subject sometimes lends itself to humour. It would be interesting to find out the original source of this particular subject. Mughal and Rajput painting both abound in it, especially in those variations where prince or princesses visit saints and their disciples, as in those pictures where Dara Shikoh is seen engaged in religious discussion. From Ajanta down to the Jaina manuscripts as well as in our folk art these visits to inspired teachers are a popular theme. In the Hindu pictures of the later period the teacher is usually an ascetic, a skeleton of a man, but in Mussalman works the divines are well-fed and portly, suggesting the ancient Indian conception, realised in the Buddha, that spiritual eminence is not inseparably associated with emaciation. Of the large number of these delightful character studies, there is probably none better than the one belonging to Jehangir's epoch in the Museum für Kunst und Gewerbe at Hamburg where Sultan Parviz is seen sitting under a tree, which divides the picture into two panels, with two benign teachers, one holding a book in his hand and the other, hunched up beside him, looking at the prince with amused tolerance. The gleam in his eyes is so different from the cold glitter we are accustomed to in those who make of religion a profession in our days! There are two outstanding single portraits belonging to Shahjehan's time of dervishes, remarkable for their delicate drawing and for the uncanny insight into their religious trends, the one of Shah Bari of Shahjehanabad representing the erudite *salik* and the other of a *majzub* forgetful of the self, concentrated with his whole being on the other world.

The meeting of divines became so popular a subject because compositionally it offered a problem for the spacing of seated figures in the midst of varying landscapes. Its other attraction was that it offered scope for the treatment of psychological traits; the identity of the painter with the inner life of his model became worth achieving after acquaintance with European painting. Moreover, how tired most of these artists must have been of always depicting the ceremonials of court life and the whims of their masters. In my view this particular picture arrangement must have become a cliché with the Indian painters and being popular with themselves as well as their patrons, even when the theme was varied, the composition was conserved. A very expressive example of this is a picture of ecstatic musicians by Bichtir, a Hindu painter of the mid xvii century with a startling gift for characterisation.

Of all the themes, however portraiture must be considered as the most significant realisation of the Mughal genius. It must be remembered that Mughal art is not one of those large roads along which the human creative spirit has travelled. At its best, it is a flowering wayside, a track that leads through pleasant fields, a delight for connoisseurs, such as are Chinese jade, or Limoges enamels or the ivories of Cordova. It has never been involved in large passions or the tragedy of destiny. Nevertheless, few examples can be found in the world's art of such unruffled tact and refined sensibility as the Mughal portraits. And if Mughal art will live in man's memory it will be for its architecture and its portraits. The Persians too had great portraitists. Amongst them were Bihzad and his followers, Sultan Muhammad, Kamel and Riza-i-Abbasi, to name the best known among them. Portraiture develops in time of peace, and the early Timurid princes had little time from their wars to pose for pictures in the manner of their descendants, Akbar and Jehangir, who in the midst of military activities had enjoyed moments of respite. Nevertheless we have a remarkable portrait of Timur himself in a coat of mail with a helmet coming deep over his face, where the beauty is not in the line but in the skilful handling of masses, which is so characteristic of Turkish work but uncommon in Persian painting. Under the Safavids a great fillip was given to portrait making and we have a ms. dated 1537 where Shah Tahmasp is seen figuring in some role or other in most of the illustrations. An interesting portrait is that of Abdullah Khan, painted about 1570, exhibiting a masterly grasp of the theme, in which this Turkestan ruler is seen holding up a melon, that loved fruit of the Central Asians, the absence of which, among other things, made Babur deprecate the civilization of India.

But Mughal portraiture stands much higher. To my mind never before or after has there been such shrewd psychological observation, realised with such economy of detail and so summarily treated, as during the best period of Mughal art. We know of no brush that was plied with greater surety and restraint, with such reticence and eloquence at the same time. A very slight pencil-shading, a quiet contour and we are face to face with a bared human destiny. Compositionally the postures are the most elementary, the hand of the model resting on the hilt of a sword, or holding a flower and yet in the stance there is no feeling of rigidity or unease. No wonder that both Rembrandt and Joshua Reynolds were so struck with its excellence. To me the most interesting are those where the outline is left as originally drawn, without use of colours. These wonderful portraits make the Mughal court relive for us in a more intimate manner than any other period of Indian history and it is due to them that we know so well those men of piety, taste, learning and valour who founded and maintained that glorious Empire.

One thing they have in common with all the best portraits of Asiatic art. They are individual portraits and at the same time they represent types. This trait is of India origin; we are supported by the fact that most of the best portraitists at the Mughal court were of Hindu origin, such as, Chitarman, Anupchater,

Govardhan, Hunhar, to name a few. There seems little doubt that many of the figures of kings and notables at Ajanta were authentic portraits drawn from living human beings exhibiting this same mixture of the particular and the ideal and displaying an unrivalled breadth of conception and execution. It is often said that Mughal art is mere book illustration and in this respect is contrasted with the Rajput, in which, also miniatures, have the character of frescoes. In other words Rajput painting, like western or Asiatic art, should be viewed diagonally or in a straight line whereas Mughal art, being folio pictures, have to be pored over in the manner of books. This contrast may hold good for the rest of Mughal work, but the portraits satisfy the same standard as the Rajput miniatures and can at will be enlarged to impressive wall-pictures. These portraits possess, in spite of their small size, especially in the Durbar scenes, which was an innovation of the Mughals, a monumentality and quiet dignity that can compare with the best figure studies in Indian art.

Passing from the subject matter to the nature of the art itself, it is here where we find the Mughals closest allied to the Persians and farthest removed from Indian tradition. It is of the utmost importance to understand this point clearly, for this is where the real line of demarcation lies which divides Mughal art from that produced at Hindu courts during the Mughal supremacy of India. Like the Persian, Mughal art is a closed, eclectic, aristocratic art, a growth of luxury and leisure, a product for the delight of the cultivated eye, without any democratic folk appeal. Rajput work, too, was produced in feudal courts or camps, but its chief subject matter was so closely connected with the marvellous, colourful outburst of religious feeling which followed in the wake of Vaishnavism that it lent itself easily to the admiration of the masses. It was boisterous, imaginative, full of the unexpected, intensely personal. This difference is due to something very deep, to racial tastes hearkening back to distant ages, to temperaments differently moulded at the beginning of civilization by religion and its handmaid, literature. It seems to me that the common source of literary forms and those of the figurative arts in Asia, the similar artistic attitude which gave rise to both, is a significant fact which has not yet been studied. It will be interesting, for example, to discover to what extent the structural serenity of the frescoes at Ajanta is derived from the same fount as the clarity and simplicity of the *jataka* stories. For a long time the historians of art have traced the tastefulness and restraint of the Persian artist and his flowing line to the practice of *nastaliq* calligraphy and have compared his execution with the freer brushwork of the Chinese painter, who also learnt his fundamental strokes from the characters of his language. This observation supplies at valuable and revealing insight into the origins of national technique. But till now little thought has been given to the analogy between the epic, the *qasida*, the *ghazal* and the style of the Persian artist. This point need not be elaborated, nor parallels brought from other Asiatic art centres, but it seems clear that most of the Mughal art in its preciosity, meticulousness and even monotony, and more particularly in its intentions, is perfectly intelligible only to those who know of that tendency of Persianised Indians, both Hindus and Mussalmans, to find their literary delight in the couplet. The couplet is limited in range; but it is pithy, aphoristic and replete with content. Its very structure makes it undemocratic and apart, a joy for dilettantes. It has not the lilt which lifts the heart, it does not unmake and remake the world as great romantic poetry does, but it is graceful and charming and, what is more important, wholly adequate. In new couplets, because of the limit imposed by its form on the number of words that may be employed, a simile tersely expressed which has been found satisfying in earlier writings, is frankly incorporated without acknowledgment. Refinement of senses and tastefulness is thus communicated from generation to generation. This is exactly what Mughal art did, for it borrowed unashamedly from its predecessors felicitous renderings without even troubling to attempt at originality. This is what the Persians did throughout their most creative epoch in painting; the manner and the feeling differing as the inspiration which produced the epic or the *rubayiat* inflamed the artist. One can even imagine the man who takes up an album of Mughal pictures and finds joy in them, to be in the same physical and mental attitude as when he bends over a collection of Indo-Persian verses. It is not claimed that the couplet was the prevalent literary form during the entire period of Mughal rule; but that a parallel might be established between the different phases through which Indo-Persian literature has passed and the development of Mughal painting which began with the tumult of battle scenes and fantastic adventures and settled down to the narrowness and perfection of the portrait. In fact, it must be clearly understood that no attempt is being made here to establish the influence of literary forms on the figurative arts. That would be a disparagement of our mediaeval art products which no student of art dare allow himself. The laws that govern literary products are quite distinct from those which govern art products. If this were not so art objects would have no claim to an independent existence. The greatest drawback of the early discussions on our art has been this very unwarranted interpretation of the one with the help of the other. What I am pointing out is merely resemblances in forms, which exist parallelly at one and the same time, and that these forms evolve from a general cultural conception of life. The resultant attitude towards the facts of the universe rules their rise and growth and begets analogous styles. Similarly it may be argued that Rajput art was a reflection of a great epic and lyrical tradition. It was a romantic art, distinct in character but not in technique from Mughal art, with a larger sweep of imagination corresponding to a larger variety and range of contemporary literary forms. Those who know the songs of mediaeval Indian poets and saints, unconscious of their burden of beauty, naïve and unadorned, ecstatical and tender, will get a true glimpse of the feeling which inspired this art. It is Krishna-lila, it is Kabir, Mira Bai and Vidyapati in line and colour.

II

Until now we have been considering some traits of Persian art which influenced the Mughals; I have tried to indicate the individual contributions of the Mughals and mentioned their indigenous attachments and alliances and touched upon a few of the similarities and differences existing between the Mughal and the Persian, on the one side, and, on the other, between the Mughal and mediaeval Hindu art. This last point requires elaboration because the approach is controversial and rests on contentions which have not been accepted by the more well-known writers on Indian art, who have been most assiduous in dissociating Mughal art from the Rajput, maintaining the superiority of the latter over the former—a vain attempt, for beauty has many facets—and have tried to trace Rajput painting to purely indigenous influences.

It is well-known that after Ajanta we have no certain records of great painting in India till its revival in the xvi century. Attempts have therefore been made to fill up this hiatus, and since Ajanta, like Buddhism, which inspire it, is not merely an Indian but an Asiatic heritage, we have been told to look beyond our frontiers for the survival of Indian traditions, to Central Asia, to China and to Japan. But painting followed in these countries the line of the evolution of a national art which assimilated foreign influences; it was never imitative. The Indian influence is obviously undeniable; but it was so deeply modified by counter-influences, Turki, Scythian and Chinese, that the resemblance between the paintings of those countries and our own mediaeval work is indeed remote. As this was undisputed it was postulated that Indian painting must have had a continuous existence in India, the records of which have been lost to us, lurking perhaps somewhere in mountain fastnesses, in forgotten provincial courts or in religious confraternities. Then the newly-discovered Gujerati Jaina miniatures were taken to be the missing link connecting Ajanta and Rajput work. Hindu or Rajput mediaeval painting, as is well-known, is divided into two groups—Rajasthani and Pahari, and it has been claimed that this division has been made solely for convenience of classification. The difference, however, in the nature of the two schools, in feeling and in the methods of solving the pictorial problems, is immense. Except that both deal with analogous subjects, the line of demarcation between them is as clearly and deeply marked as between themselves and Mughal art. The fact that Hindu painters were responsible for their production is of no particular significance since much of Mughal painting was also the work of Hindus. A common religion professed by artists is hardly enough to unite such disparate artistic expressions into one group. For the same reason, because Jaina work was done by Hindus and was inspired by Hindu religious traditions it is not necessarily allied to pictures painted in other Hindu cultural groups. Whoever has seen the Jaina miniatures, their stolid composition, their crude contrasting colours, their dullness and stiffness, cannot possibly maintain that it was they that paved the way to that work, vibrant with life and colour, which was produced in Rajasthan and in the Hills. The utmost that might be conceded is that the firm, though unimaginative, drawing which underlay Jaina work and the iconographical types to which it gave currency may, to some extent, have influenced early Rajasthani painting, as can be seen in the picture of a saint from Rajputana of the early xvii century, but it had no effect at all on the Kangra school. In fact, when you compare Jaina miniatures with Mola Ram's work or with other Hill paintings, you will be convinced that, if at all, they had a very restricted sphere of radiation, and although outwardly there may be points of similarity, even Rajasthani work of the best kind is absolutely unaffected by these drawings of marionettes with sharp pointed noses in two-third profiles.

It would be useful to consider briefly the character of the interesting Rajasthani school of painting, which grew and flourished in the Rajputana plains and which was one of the three important movements in the Indian art of the middle ages. So much has been made of the undisputed charm and excellence of the works of the Hindu Hill painters with their easy communicability and quick, sensuous appeal that due attention has not been paid to Rajasthani painting, perhaps a little unsympathetic to the casual observer, but in essence vigorous and expressionistic. Roughly speaking, this school has two epochs, the earlier being dramatic and gestural and the later, under court influence, tending to become hieratic and crudely lyrical. Crudeness is one of the glaring traits of this work, but such is the forcefulness of expression that the very defect becomes a virtue. In fact, in sentiment and technique, it is nearest to modernist art movements because, like them, it encounters the aesthetic expectation with a blow, smashing it and then re-piecing it into an experience of its own. This will be evident from a striking picture from the xvi century representing one of the *ragas* reproduced by Coomaraswamy in his standard book on *Indian and Indonesian Art*, a close study of which will reveal to you the principles of this art.* Though at first glance the composition appears simple, much ingenuity has been expended by the artist in order to justify pictorially the horizontal gesture of the arm of the seated figure. This unseeming, effortless shrewdness in one of the characteristics of folk art, and early Rajasthani pictures in many respects approximate that kind of art. The sentiment is simple and naïve, but the execution determined and audacious, unconscious and unafraid of critical standard, which prevail in sophisticated milieus and which impose on an artist's creation hesitancy and nervousness. The stylisation of the tree with clambering 'sappy' leaves appears in a form which must have become a popular convention since it is to be found persisting in may pictures of a much later date.

Perhaps with some show of justification it may be maintained of this school that, taking as it does its root in the Indian soil, rich in folk traditions and gestural in the bold spirit of Indian sculpture, it is independent of outside influence; but this would be a superficial observation, for, on closer scrutiny, it will be found that Rajasthani work, though to a lesser extent than Hill art, also belongs to the Indo-Persian family The first thing one

---

* Plate lxxxiii.

should notice is that the colouring has the same quality as in Persian painting, and, what is more, the technique of emphasising different planes with the use of lustrous colours, which is one of the characteristics of Bihzad's school, is also employed here. The palette of the artist, except in the black and the beautiful Indian red, which are obviously indigenous, is un-Indian, the ingredients used the same as in the list of Persian and Mughal colours and prepared in exactly the same manner. The enamel-like surface of the pictures brings this school and the best works of Kangra nearer to the Persians in colouring, than the art of the Mughals. One fact, however, is absolutely certain that Jaina miniatures could have had no influence at all on the colour scheme of these artists.

The trees on the left of the picture also deserve attention; the first cypress nearest the extended arm is obviously an Islamic contribution.* Trees with bulbous leaves figure more often in Rajasthani work; they are frequently met with in the folk art of most peoples. We find them as far apart as Bengal *pats* and the Russian *luboks*. In very early Persian art, before Mongol influence had opened up for it new directions, we find the same kind of tree, evidently derived from Arab Mesopotamia. There are several pictures of the period of the Abbasids where such trees figure. In one of them there are birds among the leaves. The tree, as is well-known, is an ancient Iranian symbol, being the representation of Homa, the tree of life. It occurs in that context in almost all the classical arts. The birds seated among its branches derive from the ancient Iranian legend of the singing tree. Rajasthani art has many pictures with this particular decorative detail. It is not suggested that the use of the tree shows a direct Persian influence, because the tree is found in nature everywhere and as a symbol is common to all the peoples of Iranian stock, especially among the Central Asian nomads from whom the Rajput descend. It seems to me, however, that bulbous leaves with seated birds is an importation of a later date, contemporary with

---

* *Cf*, the stylised cypress in the House of Sidi Yousuf Adami at Cairo, reproduced in the classical work of Prise d' Avennes.

Mughal art, and that it was most probably borrowed from some early Persian book illustration.

My choice of examples having been limited to your text-books I shall refer to another startling picture* also symbolising one of the *ragas*, where the body is treated with that imaginative grasp of plastic forms which was the secret not only of the great masters of Indian sculpture but of those unknown inventors of the patterns for human figures which obtain in our folk art till today. But here I desire to draw your attention to another point, to the posture of the human figure stretched out at full length on the bed. It is well-known that during the Renaissance the reclining man or woman was treated iconographically in one particular attitude: the back used to be propped up on pillows or some other support and the head was on a definitely higher level than the stretched body. In fact, in many specimens the upper part of the body is drawn at almost a right angle to the lower part. In all cases, however, the feet point in the same direction as the head. This pose is exemplified in innumerable pictures depicting the birth of Christ or of John the Baptist. In instances of our own sculpture, such as the Dream of Maya or the one popularly known as the Birth of Krishna, we come across analogous attitudes. The colossal statuaries of the reclining Buddha in Eastern Asia as well as in Ceylon are treated somewhat differently as the figures lie completely on one side, but in these cases, too, the head is much above the level of the feet, which always point outwards in the same direction as the head. A notable example of this last pose is said to be the huge Ranganadhan in the holy of holies of Srirangam. The two postures described above must have been deduced from universally accepted formulae, varied as the figure lay straight or completely on the side. We notice this in an illustrated Persian ms. of the Shah-nameh belonging to the xv century, now in the possession of the Royal Asiatic Society, London; in that exquisite scene where Tahamina enters Rustem's room to find the hero plunged in thought, he is portrayed as lying at full length with

* Coomaraswamy: Plate lxxxvi.

his bead supported on his arm, the head being on a definitely higher level than the rest of the body. It is only in later Persian art, contemporary with our mediaeval painting, that we first come across the figure extended in full, twisted at the waist with the feet pointing to a direction opposed to the movement of the head and sometimes to the upper part of the body. There is a picture of a lady reclining by the riverside, reproduced by Martin from the Collection Claude Anet,* attributed to the end of the xvi century, supposed to have been drawn by Shah Quli, where we find this cliché adapted for his own purposes by the Rajput painter.

On another page, Coomaraswamy gives us the illustration of a Jammu picture of the xvii century depicting the siege of Lanka.†

The hill-side is peopled with monkeys who listen to the important conversation taking place in the middle of the picture among human beings. It is amusing to contrast the solemn and responsible attitude of these monkeys with a Mughal illustration of the Anwar-i-Sohaili of Akbar's time in which the same love of animals and observation of their plastic possibilities is manifested, but where they are depicted in a playful mood. I do not suggest any influence of one picture on the other, but it is interesting to observe the tendency in Indian artists to invest animals with human qualities and in the Persians to infuse into human beings the sprightly litheness and untowardness of animals. A careful student of Persian art will notice, for instance, how the antelope has been utilised not only as a model for the external details of the figures of boys and women but also for their suppleness and plasticity. Rajasthani art, more often than not, strikes a portentous note but in Kangra we meet again the Persian love for moulding human figures in terms of sympathetically observed animal life. This particular picture has, however, been cited for another reason: the undisputable Persian

* *The Miniature Painting of Persia, India and Turkey*, London, 1912, Vol. II, Pl. 119b.

† Plate lxxxvii, fig. 266.

landscape in the Jammu picture of the smaller hill, with its cypresses as well as the Persian convention of the xvi century, often adopted by the Mughals for the shape and the division of the larger hill. The sea too derives from a manner introduced by the Mongols, which one notices in those rare pictures where seas figure in Persia down to the xvi century.

Jammu is one of the centres of Hill painting but the school best known and worthiest of appreciation is the one which had its home in the Kangra valley. Whilst Rajasthani art is founded on hard, manly lines with a vigorous message, here there is fluency and emotional intensity. No two schools dealing with a similar subject matter stand so far apart. To illustrate the nature of Kangra work and its character of cultured folk art, to which it contributes but from which it is not derived, one might take the famous picture of the late xviii century of homing cows, which used to belong formerly to Dr Coomaraswamy and is now at the Boston Museum. The draughtsmanship here is of the most sensitive and the treatment of the pictorial elements is so refined as to elevate it to the level of genius. Kangra is best known for its sinuous lines, for a brushwork much freer and bolder than of the Mughals but of the same calligraphical nature, manifestly more lyrical in intention and, in the majority of cases, more brilliant in execution. The colouring in the pictures of the xviii and xix centuries is Persian and some of the decorative elements are traceable to the same source. Attention may be paid on this count to a Kangra picture of the end of the xviii century in the British Museum.* The central figure holding in her right hand a scarf extended behind her belongs to the type loved of the later Kangra painters: short-statured with a drooping nose, elongated eyes and a broad face in profile. Two balustrades, also largely used by the Mughal painters, one in the foreground and the other to divide the picture into two, are of Persian origin. But the most striking borrowing is that of the leafless flowering tree at the

* Reproduced among others, by Stchoukine, Pl. xcv (a), entitled 'The Lady with a Red Shawl.'

righthand corner, a frequent decorative feature in Kangra pictures, from the Timurids and Bihzad.

Coomaraswamy says that these pictures in the bazar of Amritsar are known as 'tibati.' There is probably more in this than mere ignorance of their origin. The felicitous brushwork of this school, the lines rounding off the image in an accelerated tempo, seem to be due to the influence of China which had penetrated directly to these hill regions from the North and indirectly through Persian painting, of which the quick elastic line is also one of the most valued acquisitions. The art of Kangra, therefore, because of influences from devious routes, is more akin to the Persian and the Mughal than it is to the Rajasthani, though in some of the earlier pictures there is some resemblance between the expressive art of the Rajputs and the Himalayan painters, before they had attained to perfection of technique and come into their own in the xix century at Kangra.

When analogies and frank borrowings from Persia may be maintained in the Hills, it is the more natural that there should exist much resemblance between Rajasthani work and that of the Mughals, since both these branches of Indo-Persian painting grew in action and reaction to each other. That Mughal painting is founded on Persian conventions is undisputed; therefore, Hindu work when it is analogous to it cannot claim to have had an entirely individual life. Innumerable examples may be adduced from the books I have chosen for your convenience as being readily available to prove the resemblance. Take, for instance, the famous Jaipur cartoon of the xviii century depicting the head of the Dancing Krishna. The drawing here is extremely simple and synthetic which would appear to be a particularity of Hindu technique. Besides, the use of large decorative ornaments on the dress and headgear assimilates the picture to a placard, a kind of art foreign to the Mughals, who avoided large-sized drawing. Yet we find that this picture, and there are many of its kind, possesses a counterpart in an earlier work under Aurangzeb by Muhammad Afzal which depicts a young Gujrati woman. The cliché seems to have been in vogue, both amongst Hindus and the Mughals, before the Rajput painter of Krishna attempted his masterly work. The same can be said of the pictures from the Heroine series, which was a theme loved of Rajput artists.

In this connection one might notice the night scenes which abound in the work of Hindu painters. A peculiar convention is used: though there is darkness all around, the faces of the personages are as visible as by daylight. It is argued that this is an Indian innovation, and is often used to prove the disregard by Hindus of realistic situations. As a matter of fact, in almost all of these pictures, and some of them were also done in Mughal courts, there is always a light thrown from lanterns, torches, the moon, zigzag lightning, to illumine the faces, so that a justification of the visibility is attempted. This claim of the historians of Hindu art is not quite maintainable. The Persians had employed this convention earlier and it was from them that Indian mediaeval art borrowed it. In the same ms. of the Shah-nameh of the xv century, to which I have referred, there is a picture of Rustem rescuing Bizhan from a dungeon. The hero is standing at its mouth looking down into it and a block arbitrarily removed at the bottom of the picture reveals the prisoner, reduced to a skeleton, but visible in every detail as in stark daylight. This, too, is a night scene which is suggested by a cluster of stars and the young moon. Though every face is clearly visible, there still lurks in the texture of the landscape a sense of a cold deep darkness. The defiance of realism is one of those deliberate escapes which great artists in all climes have sought in order to obtain an untrammelled scope for their creation.

It seems to me that to maintain the utter independence of Hindu art from the Persian is a striking instance of how cultural history is sometimes confused by narrowness and sentimentality. The advent of the Mughals was as momentous for the mediaeval art of India as that of the Kushans for the classical period. It opened the way for international contacts, broke up dry traditionalism, introduced a creative leaven into Indian life. Mughal tolerance, reasonableness and tact founded an appropriate atmosphere for the growth of the arts. Theirs was an epoch for revelations and recognitions. The significance accorded to painting in the Mughal court, a Timurid tradition (for, even in Timur's time, the most highly-prized present to the conqueror was a Chinese picture), caused the feudal Hindu houses, whether aligned with or against the new dynasty, to extend patronage to their artists and craftsmen. Moreover, paper of different kinds for painting was introduced by the Mughals from Persia and this comparatively uncostly material gave the Rajput artists a fruitful opportunity for experimentation which was denied to them by the very nature of frescoes. Specific Persian pigments, such as the blues of lapis lazuli and the yellows of orpiment, were also imported from that country and the depth and liveliness of Rajput colouring, except where the origin is frankly indigenous as during the 'barbaric' period of the Plains painting, allies the latter to the Persians more than to the Mughals, who employed soberer colours. The greatest contribution of the Persians to Hindu art, however, besides the accelerated line which might also have been derived from folk art, was the communication of a sense of design, of the preconceived pictorial design. The Persians are amongst the great masters of design in the world and the complete control of the pictorial rhythm by the Rajputs under most difficult conditions is to be traced to their example, since Jaina work deals with static situations and is therefore stereotyped and iconographical.

At this point it is necessary to clear up the different connotations the word 'influences' has in art history. The most easily perceivable influences are in the cases of copies or adaptations of identical themes with great resemblances in the representation. Few instances of these occur among the objects that have attained the status of art. Influences are also detected when certain decorative details, such as, cypresses, large beads, bulbous leaves, etc., or decorative arrangements, such as the Persian garden, rectangular carpets, etc., are transported from one art group to another in recognisable shapes. The former point to an adoption of objects of material civilization which is of more interest to archaeology than to art; the latter reveal the use of certain conventions which have been deemed pleasurable and artistically satisfactory. This last is of the domain of art history. Within this class also fall those realisations in plasticity, such as, the woman in a lying position, which one cultural group borrows from the iconography of another. All these, summed up in the words ornaments and motifs, are easily visible to the eye and when such influences are pointed out there can be no doubt of their validity. Art history, however, is more intimately concerned with the problem of forms, their conception and realisation. Now, forms have no meaning unless they are exteriorised in space with the help of adequate technique. Significant form is the artist's vision reduced to line, colour, movement in the best possible way. At the moment of creation the artist is one with the object to be created and with his material and yet he is himself and the object is itself; he is aware of the externality of the object and at one and the same time is conscious of his capacity of translating his vision by technical means into form. So influences of technique are more important than ornaments or motifs as they make an incursion into the very nature of the art. When we say that an Indian artist paints under European influence we do not mean that we find in his pictures European furniture of European decorative ornaments only. We mean that the structure of his forms, the disposition of his pictorial elements, the means he employs for realising his artistic purpose, are European. The subject matter of a picture is no indication of style or school. Europeans may paint Indians; the Persians and the Mughals did paint a number of Europeans. The Hindus, on the other hand, filled their pictures with architectural and floral elements with which they were most familiar. Their themes, too, were drawn from their mythology and legends; the ethnical types they painted belong to the regions where they flourished. But their manner of realisation, whether in the technique of the laying of colours, in the cohesion of design where all fantasy and truculence was subjected to a disciplined pictorial end and even in the structure of their forms was Persian. You will notice that on all counts, though they be of varying degrees of importance for art history, Rajput art stands a debtor to Persia.

Why should the recognition of foreign influences be a disparagement of any art? There is no great art in the world, however individual it might appear at first sight, the Chinese, the Achaemenian or the Egyptian, which is not composite and where other races have not contributed to its development. A virile artistic milieu absorbs foreign influences and adapts them to its own needs, impressing on them the hall-mark of its national genius. It is only at the beginning, or in effete societies, that foreign influences have a disintegrating effect. One can go further and maintain that all authentic art with an intense human appeal must necessarily be the product of several counteracting influences. Because I believe in this, I have attempted to focus your attention on three branches of Indo-Persian art which came into being as the result of the collaboration of the two great peoples of India and which an enlightened organic society of patrons and connoisseurs have left to us as one of the most exquisite legacies of our past.

4

A Nation's Art

I

Before dealing with the main theme of my talk, it may not be out of place to speak to you about the word 'Art,' which figures in its title. In common speech art is an extremely elastic and vague term apt to be applied to such varied human activities as painting, cooking, to the way that one makes up one's face, or even to the manner of telling lies. Common speech, however, is a reflection of common sense and the essential meaning of this word, as understood by specialists, is not so very different from what it connotes in everyday use. For, in both cases, it suggests skill in the attainment of an end and implies a sort of perfection when that end had been attained. In the language of those who have made a special study of art, the word for the various ways in which skill is applied is 'technique' and that for the various shapes which the attempt at perfection assumes is 'form.' Art objects, thus, are the union of these two, technique and form, and art study consists in following their evolution, their interrelation and interdependence. The one cannot exist without the other; technique, which fails to realise satisfactorily the intuitively apprehended or the preconceived form, proves incapacity in dealing with the material of art, whether it be stone, voice or the human body; form, however marvellous in conception, is a chimera of the brain unless reduced to something tangible, audible, or visible.

What objects then produced by human endeavour can be called works of art? What are their essential characteristics and how are they to be distinguished from other objects? Or in other words, why is the status of art accorded to a certain category of objects and denied to others? The answer to these questions must be very complicated and I shall try to give it to you in as simple language as possible. The difficulty in ascribing, let us say, a picture to 'art' is about the same as when one calls verses 'literature.' Art criticism finds itself involved in the same difficulties as literary criticism. In both cases attempts have been made to find certain objective standards; but basing oneself on common experience, it has been maintained that we like a poem or a picture mainly because of its appeal to our personal emotions. Nevertheless, the quest of art (the word is employed here in its narrower application to the figurative arts) and of literary criticism is of great importance, because after the elimination of the subjective element, we discover that our tastes react more or less uniformly to poems or pictures, which possess certain inherent virtues. One of these, and probably the most important, is that quality which makes us feel the technique to be perfectly adequate to the realised form. In the case of a poem, this would mean that the succession of words, their significance and their movement, which we call rhythm, are the best possible for the expression of the emotion, which is the subject matter of the poem. In painting, we would say that the colours, the disposition of the pictorial elements in space, the arrangement of the parts into a pictorially intelligible whole, that is, the composition, which is a frame-work of lines and volumes in varying interrelations, have been used in the best possible manner for the expression of the painter's intention. Perfection of form has been aimed at and achieved with the help of technique.

A second characteristic of a work of art is its utter uselessness, because it is the product of a perfectly gratuitous activity in man. The first painters of pre-historic times, impelled by an urge of representation, as children are, recorded their impressions of animal life on the walls of caves. These, as in the drawings of the Altamira caves in Southern Europe, show a keenness of observation and a mastery of the expressive yet economical line such as has been rarely surpassed by later painters in civilized society. This work was perfectly useless but not purposeless. The contrast between these two expressions should be noticed. The primitive man believed in the magic quality of his drawings and hoped that the animals he represented would fall a prey to him and satisfy his hunger; the only preoccupation of man in these very early days being the fulfilment of this one need. So it might well be asked if the primitive man had a purpose, why should his activity be termed gratuitous. You would be in good company, for no less a person than Aristotle divided the arts into utilitarian and non-utilitarian, putting under the first head cooking, architecture, etc., and under the second music, sculpture and dancing, in so far as the last is for the delight of the eye and not for bodily exercise. At first sight, Aristotle's contention appears correct and the view about the utter uselessness of the arts seems to be an unjustifiable straining after originality, for how can one affirm that cooking which is for the purpose of feeding us, or architecture, which is for housing us, is useless? One may go further and argue that even music, sculpture and dancing serve a useful social purpose because they afford us pleasure and distraction. These are indisputable facts. Nevertheless, on close scrutiny, it will be found that cooking and architecture, viewed as fine arts, do but incidentally fulfil their utilitarian ends. The chief aim of fine cooking is to afford pleasure to the palate and not to fill the stomach; that of architecture is to satisfy our sense of proportion and decoration, to delight us by the architect's inventiveness in so deftly solving the problem of limited space as to meet our housing needs and in placing our buildings in a satisfactory relation to the surrounding landscape. His activity is of the same nature as of the Indian or the Chinese potter, who produces things of beauty that serve a useful purpose; in the process of the making, however, though the element of usefulness is ever present in his mind, his being, if he is an artist, is concentrated on the creation of a form, which would impart a quick feeling of pleasure. It is obvious that a pleasure-giving form has no reference to man's practical needs in the future, being exclusively for immediate contemplation and enjoyment in the fast-dissolving present. It is this feature of works of art, which distinguishes an artist's achievements from those of a scientist. Had an artist never existed, material civilisation would have still gone on. We would still have had houses and cooking pots. Even in our conduct there would have been little difference, for we would have conformed exclusively to religious and social demands. Only the flush of joy at the sight of beauty, which makes us live keenly and sensitively, would have been absent. The exigent aesthetic expectation, the satisfaction of which is a need as urgent as any in the moral world, have been left unfulfilled.

A third reason why a given object is classed as a work of art is to be found in the fact that is has the sanction of history behind it. From time immemorial we have sensed, even when we have been unable to express it clearly, that certain objects conform to our taste. In other words, by their shapes they satisfy our feeling for beauty because they come up to certain standards evolved in the course of the historical development of our country, our community or our social group. These objects represent traditions that have stood the test of time and have been found aesthetically satisfactory. The community has groped amidst varying forms, which nature suggests, and settled on particular ones as answering to something very deep and indefinable, to a vision of beauty connected darkly and intimately with its blood, its geographical environments, its peculiar historical destiny. This particular vision of beauty of a cultural group gives rise to what may be called a nation's art; the word 'nation' is being used here to mean not a political but a cultural unit. Now, of all the words in any language beauty is the least capable of definition or description. In fact, it is this very quality of indefinability which constitutes the essence of beauty. Beauty has many aspects, and each nation has chosen the one aspect which most fulfils its aesthetic need in the same way as, after experiments, it has fixed on specific national dishes to satisfy its appetite. The choice in both cases has been made with due regard to climatic, geographical and social factors and in conformity with the lines along which a particular national civilisation has grown. But as we have individual preferences for certain kinds of food, hunger being a need capable of being fulfilled in many ways, so individuals and nations have preferences for certain forms to satisfy their aesthetic hunger. Beauty is therefore not the exclusive possession of any one cultural group. Whenever the aesthetic activity has achieved success, that is, whenever the technique was completely adequate to the ends it desired to achieve, beauty had its birth. If you understand this you will realise how unreasonable it is to place the art of one nation over that of another. Unfortunately, it was the general practice of art historians, till about thirty years ago, to rank the art products of nations as they approximated to the Greek ideal of beauty or fell short of it. There can be no doubt that the Greeks, because of the masterly treatment and high quality of their sculpture of the best age, hold a pre-eminent position in the history of art. In the surface and the texture of their work they have been rarely surpassed. As they were concerned mostly with the beauty of the human body, their art is intelligible and easily appreciated. If you analyse the praise that is lavished on them, and which they richly deserve, you will find that the appreciation is due to the fact that they have been successful in attaining their end, which, in their case, was a particular conception of the human form, with the help of a perfectly adequate technique. We have thus always to seek the end particular cultural groups have in view and the manner of its realisation before we can speak of the excellence or otherwise of works of art. It is rash to attempt to define the ends which nations have aimed at attaining in their art. Yet a cursory view of the world's art will convince you that expression, which is the active form of beauty, differs in the products of each country. Thus, whilst the Greek desired to raise man to divinity, in Indian art we have the reverse process of dealing with gods engaged in human actions. Hence, Greek sculpture is comparatively static and Indian sculpture pre-eminently dynamic. The different ends followed define the contrasting forms of these two arts. Whilst the Greeks have treated their models with poise, restraint and an accurate knowledge of anatomy, superb in the command of technique, the Indians have achieved an amazing plasticity of form, defying anatomical limits and displaying the most adventurous possibilities of the human body. The purpose of the Egyptians was to work for eternity; the Chinese and the Persians aimed at exquisiteness and the refinement of the senses, the Iranians at monumentality. Every nation thus has a peculiar artistic profile of its own, modified and changed in some respects because of currents and cross-currents of influences, and yet true to the fundamental form, which embodies the national vision of beauty.

II

I have already discussed certain traits which characterise works of art, and mentioned that one national art differs from another according to the ends it intends to achieve and that one therefore can never maintain the superiority of the art of one cultural group over that of another. I have attempted to show that Greek art, perfect as it is in its own way, cannot be taken as a standard by which to judge the art products of countries for whom beauty meant movement, exquisiteness or monumentality. Now, the ends that a nation strives to attain result from certain conditions under which its particular civilisation has grown. These ends are limited by geographical factors, among others. For instance, in regions where there are stone quarries, sculpture is always to be found. Form, thus, is always conceived in relation to the material at hand and with regard to the difficulty or ease in the manipulation of that material. Hence, problems of technique are ever present in an artist's mind limiting the vagaries of his phantasy. The creative artist is hemmed in also by other factors, equally important. He is a member of a society and, like other member of it, a product of its evolution. He has the same preferences and prejudices as they. Whether impelled by a pure urge for artistic creation, by vanity or by commercial interest, he is obliged to take into account those standards of taste, which are embodied in a society's art traditions. Even when he is an innovator, as many modernist artists in Europe are today, he cannot escape the shackles, because he either experiments in the traditions of other countries in a spirit of eclecticism, or he attempts to create newer interrelations of lines and masses, sometimes in utter disregard of natural forms. But he is always subservient to aesthetic doctrines which are authoritative in certain social milieus composed of patrons and admirers in his own cultural group or in other groups outside with which he has affinities and in the traditions of which he participates.

The most revolutionary creative painter in his most sensational phases, when he is striving to impose on us new traditions by forcing apparently incoherent elements into a pictorial whole, is as fettered by the nature of his material and by prevailing social and economic considerations as any traditional artist. He is like those bold legendary warriors in Chinese annals who cover their faces with frightening masks and paint their bodies over with dragons in order to terrorise their opponents and effect their rout; but behind all this horrible paraphernalia there beats a delicate Chinese heart. What can be claimed for the modernist artist, whether he be a cubist, a suprematist, a naivist, a dadaist, is that he is perhaps more sensitive than others to the changes that imperceptibly are often taking place in the national taste. In this he is not so different from that much-despised philistine, the businessman, who is equally alive to the commercial advantages of newer demands. In fact, the world of art at any given period in all countries may be compared to a large furniture workshop where new shapes for chromium-plated chairs, with the seats in unexpected angles to suit the vagaries of the modern man or woman's figure, are being fabricated side by side with sofas in an ancient style appropriate to the period of crinolines and good manners. The contrast, thus, between the modernist and the traditionalist is not so very marked as is often made out to be. Both types have always existed at one and the same time in a nation's art history and both have produced works in order to supply aesthetic demands. Only one tendency has represented a more prevailing current of taste with a larger appeal, whilst the other, perhaps a more vigorous cross-current, accepted and sensed by a select few. The thing to notice is that both kinds of artists in their creative moments cannot but repose on the flowing stream of a nation's cultural life.

There is a common misconception, encouraged by modernist theorists of arts, that the so-called traditionalist is not free in his creation. But a nation's artistic tradition is of many kinds and variety and an artist always does exercise his freedom of choice in taking only that which is most suited to his temperament. You will see that within the lines laid down by tradition he can fully exercise his individual creative powers producing thereby variations of current forms. It is not necessary to roam all the seas to discover the marvels with which the world abounds; there is enough in a flowering lane to content the heart of man. The limits of traditional art have never stood in the way of a great creator impressing his individual genius on his works. You have only to look at Early Christian art, which flourished in the courts of Byzantium, to find how hieratic forms, sanctioned by religious usage, undergo variations in objects of silver, ivory, wood and chiefly in painting and mosaic, notwithstanding the decorative rigidity of their contours. You can see in the Hindu sculptures at Ellora how the dictates of iconographical texts have been observed and at the same time violated by masters who have made of these caves one of the most marvellous temples of human talent.

We have seen that both the innovator and the conservative artist depend on national traditions and contribute to national art. I have tried to show that traditions of art do not necessarily hamper creative freedom, nor do they interfere with individual expression when it is forceful and bears a message of its own. National taste in a vital society is never static; it is always changing and is being modified by internal and external influences. The thing to remember is that changes in artistic traditions in a living society do not bring about fundamental modifications of those characteristic forms, which reflect the national vision of beauty. They are more in the nature of adaptations or adoptions freely made without constraint of any kind. If the adoption takes place at a time, when society is lifeless and therefore certain art forms can be forced down on it from above, because they are invested with the glory of military conquest, they never become integral parts of a national heritage, but remain foreign and irrelevant. Take the case of Hellenistic art which, after Alexander's conquests, spread over the whole of Asia. In Gandhara and north-western Punjab it was wholly unsuccessful despite the fact that it dealt with Buddhist, that is Indian, themes, because these traditions never touched the Indian imagination. The technique and forms of Hellenistic art were adopted because it enjoyed a great prestige in Indo-Greek courts but the society that accepted it was uncreative. In Chinese art, on the other hand, where these very traditions were freely incorporated as a part of those influences, Iranian, Nomadic and Indian, which infiltrated from Central Asia, they gave remarkable results in the marvellous sculpture of the T'ang dynasty after about four centuries of Gandhara. In India itself these very Hellenistic traditions were imported to the South from Alexandria by the sea-route and accepted by a living society. The result was the stone-reliefs at Amaravati, vibrant with life and ingenuity, contrasting so favourably with the dull stereotyped work of Northern India.

It does not deprive an art of its virtue if modifications are brought about in it by foreign influences. In fact, the greater the number of influences in an art, the larger its human appeal. There are periods when national art reaches a point of deadness and debases itself into formalism. At these moments foreign conquests, bringing in their train the possibilities of international contacts, revivify it. India has been extremely fortunate in this respect. At the beginning of the Christian era when it was degenerating into discursiveness and monotony, the Kushans, a nomadic Iranian dynasty that had ruled in Bactria, appeared on the scene with a baggage of Central Asian nomadic and Hellenistic traditions and, with the help of a new set of

Buddhistic symbols, helped to create a continental art of Asiatic significance, which was founded on indigenous forms that had been overlaid by Hellenism. In our middle ages, likewise, the Mughals infused the apathy and dryness into which Indian traditions of painting had fallen with a magnificent urge and contributed to the birth of Indo-Persian art, Mughal and Rajput. It is my belief that a national art can be vigorous and effective only when it has the courage to accept freely adaptable foreign influences, and is vital enough to assimilate them to its own artistic needs.

5

The Art of Jamini Roy

An individual exhibition of the work of Jamini Roy is an event of high importance in the world of modern Indian art. Recently some of his paintings have been shown in 'omnibus' exhibitions in Calcutta and though they were given the place of prominence and honour they deserve because of their distinctive quality, the impression left with one, who had to wander through galleries encumbered with mediocre pictures, is not conducive to a proper assessment of that forceful expression which is pre-eminently his contribution to the art of today. To be able to fully appreciate his work and gain that totality of aesthetic experience which derives from a consistent ensemble, created by a talent vigorously sincere in relation to itself, one has to visit, as some of us have been privileged to do, his modest one-storied house at Baghbazar, where his large panels, in their proper setting, fulfil an almost architectonic purpose. In this exhibition one may review the entire range of his production, mark the different stages where he has tarried on his way to an undisputed *maîtrise* and discover that tenacious artistic will which he has exercised since the earliest days. No patronage came his way during the period of his struggle, when he was treated as an unlettered outlaw by oracular dilettantes, who utter final judgments on art products in our town. When recognition came, as it has today, unfortunately more for the stubborn and uncowed insistence of his artistic method than for his achievements, he is already advanced in age, a self-effacing, ineloquent man, whose most fruitful years of creation now lie behind him. No painter in India, to my knowledge, had lived in such concentrated seclusion, in such unshared communion with the object of his quest.

An artist's life amongst us today is not an easy one; in almost all cases it has to be lived in silence and discouragement, undowered by recognition, an outcast's life in which the fact that his activity, by its very nature, is gratuitous is proved to him to the hilt. How can it be otherwise? Those who have money attach no value to art products; those who would like to encourage the producers of art have no means. Even the acquisition of objects of art or its patronage, for the sake of social prestige, which is practised not only by the Europeans but was a habit in the East in places where a high bourgeoisie flourished, as at Pergamon during the Hellenistic period, or amongst us under the Sungas, to name only two instances, does not obtain any more. Moreover, as far as painting is concerned, the hanging of pictures within frames in rooms, when no organically decorative end is served, is not in the Indian tradition. Only those who live like Europeans take to it, but in their case the cheap oleographs of sentimental landscapes and especially of gross nudes, hawked in the streets of Calcutta and Bombay, are preferred to native products, more particularly if they seem to bear affinity to indigenous forms. For probably no social milieu exists anywhere in the world, which can compare with those unintelligent Indo-Anglian coteries, with which our larger towns abound, for pretentiousness and for want of sympathy and understanding. Uncultured in their tastes because they lack visual experience of the best products of either western or eastern art, nurtured in the most facile forms of lower middle class European civilisation, they are harshest in their evaluation of work like Jamini Roy's, in spite of the fact that it can be justified by modern, if not modernistic, art theories, prevalent in those very countries where they have lived lives of superficiality and Ersatz.

Under these conditions Jamini Roy has had his full share of neglect and bitterness. Few know of the vicissitudes of his career as an artist, tinged as it is with a deep personal tragedy. For years he was held to be a crank, a rebel against the Bengali revivalist movement, a fanatic in vain pursuit of originality. These accusations are not without some foundation, for as an artist he has really had momentary aberrations. He did once take up with the others painting in the Bengali School and produced pretty pictures with weak lines and sentimental colouring. It is perfectly true that he is a fanatic—relentless, narrow, intense—working with one unique aim, and that is to achieve complete control over technique for the fulfilment of his artistic ends. The path he had pursued is that of all authentic artists in all ages, and the result has been that he has reached a standard of draughtsmanship unattended by any painter in India, including the best known amongst them.

The very nature of Jamini Roy's work precludes a generality of appeal. He cannot be easily appraised by laymen, particularly as the entire trend of his life, both as an artist and as a man, has been in the direction of evading popular approval. At the same time, together with Nandalal Bose, he has always been enthusiastically admired and discussed by those who are interested in the handicraft of painting and in the forms of our cultural renaissance. He is pre-eminently an artist's painter. His more famous contemporary, both pupils—but how different?—of the most enlightened of our painters, Abanindranath Tagore, because of the variety of his technique and the larger diapason of his inspiration, has compelled even people who are generally indifferent to art to appreciate him. Nandalal Bose's paintings frequently reflect moments of our cultural preoccupations. But Jamini Roy paints in timelessness. His pursuit, so undauntedly followed, is after expressive form, shorn of uncoordinated irrelevancies, a seeking, like Cézanne's, after the inherent idea of the object distilled from its concreteness. The most valuable experiments in this exhibition point to that singular goal. No artist in Indian of our day has been so obstinately and consistently obsessed with the fundamental problems of art. His work, except in the last phase, and that too to the extent I shall indicate, is totally empty of any topical or illustrative content. It is for this reason that his admirers have always thought that once he should be afforded the opportunity to paint frescoes in a temple, built according to his own design, because, during the years of his work, he has developed an exceptional sense of the structural in art. Today he has settled on the simplest compositional scheme reminding one of the early Rajasthani painter and, like him, he has discovered the possibilities of plasticity in apparently rigid forms. Like him, too, at his best moments, he attains, with the simplest of means, to dignity and the monumental.

In his younger days, like all the students of the Calcutta School of Art of the time, he had tried his hand at European technique. This exhibition which represents all the directions he has followed has several specimens of that period. His early training in European academic tradition counts for much in the further growth of his art, though this would be refuted by some of his more enthusiastic admirers. It seems a mistake to deny the importance in the work of modern Indian artists, and even of those of an earlier date, of essays in the realistic method as an essential for that discipline and technical efficiency on which their maturer works, with another intention, are ultimately founded. Though Jamini Roy in these early pictures of his was weak in colouring, European traditional painting undoubtedly taught him that sureness of the drawn line which makes his best work live. There are also several interesting attempts at impressionism, some of them of a striking nature, as for instance, the portrait of a seated man in black clothes with a flat turban, or the European dame with a square figure where the features are not drawn. It is rarely that one sees, in India, paintings in the foreign manner of such quality. One wonders what models he had fed his eyes upon, considering that we hardly ever get, not of course the originals, but even the reproductions of contemporary work in Europe. We have to trace his understanding of the movement to a remarkable gift for intuitive insight into the doctrines lying at the base of divergent art manifestations which, equipped as he is, he is incapable of formulating or interpreting intellectually. But the indefiniteness of impressionism was alien to Jamini Roy's temperament; what he acquired from it was the knowledge of the suggestiveness of shapes, economy and, above all, the habit of rapidly fixing on the contours of nascent ideas before they became stale and formless.

On further acquaintance with modern movements in Europe he must have come to know the post-impressionists and Picasso, also perhaps by chance, for some of his pictures of that period are reminiscent of them, particularly of Picasso of the epoch, which he had left balancing between the fascination of popular illustrations and the religious *pathétique*, and entrenched himself in the generous classical line, almost unbearably intensified by the use of a single tint. To the post-impressionists, apart from a rigid selectiveness and an austere elimination of the unnecessary, he is linked by never being able to leave the representational for the schematic. As much as they, he is enshackled by the inevitable coherence of natural appearance, even at those moments when the vibrant line would suggest the urge to repiece appearance in pictorially a more significant design. That temptation has surely been his, as it had been of the post-impressionists, especially of the early Dérain of the period of the red, brown and black outline, with whom, unknown to himself, he has many affinities, but neither of them dared wholly to yield to it because of a survival of academism in the consciousness, even at the freest moments of creation. This, of course, is also in consonance with Indian tradition, which always governs him, for, in Indian art too, in spite of the shrewdest manipulation of mass and volume, there never was a complete liberation from the interconnections of natural forms. Jamini Roy has also never deviated from that practice of the post-impressionists to derive beauty from the beauty residing in the subject. But where he differs most from them is in his unabating love for surface and outline. Using the colours and the brush that he does and employing the technique most appropriate to his characteristic works, he never attempted to experiment in the approaching and receding planes, produced by short and strong strokes of the brush, which is the glory of the post-impressionists. In his latest phase, in pictures, such as the *Village Minstrels*, where dim outline figures are dominated by

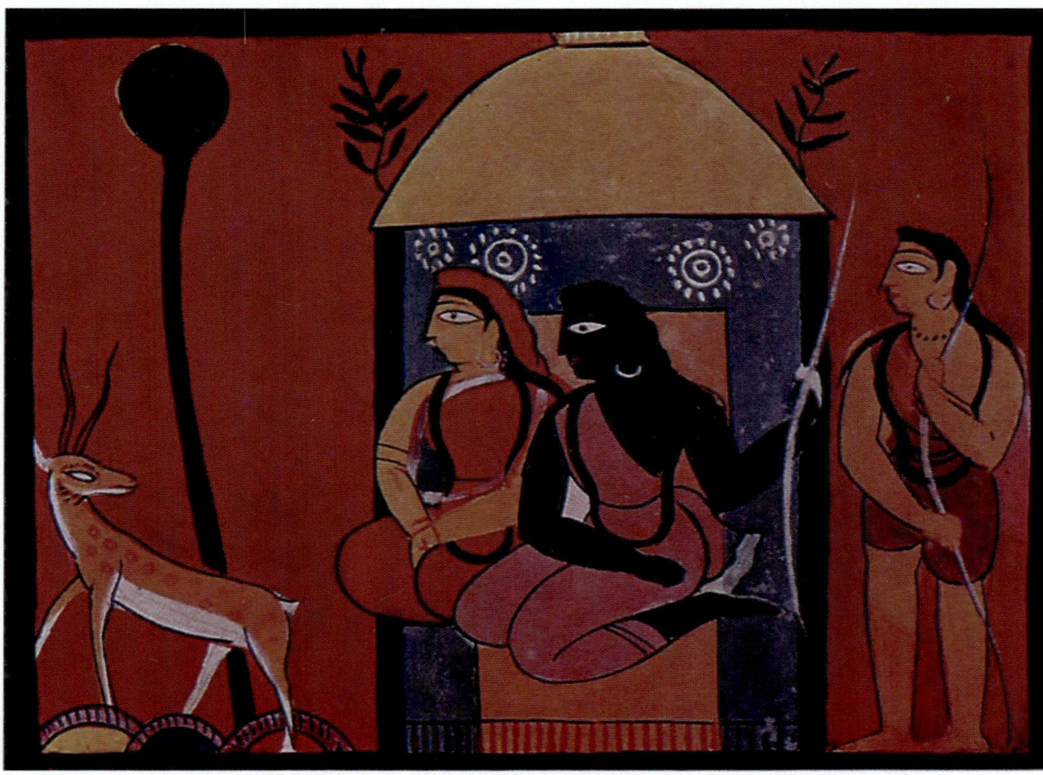

Rama, Lakshman and Sita (from the Ramayana series) by Jamini Roy, 20" x 14".

an unforgettable face on a stilted body, surging from amidst them, he has tried to achieve this very effect of related planes but not with quite satisfactory results. This is a pity, for, knowing his gift for concrete expression, one is constrained to accuse him of having sacrificed, for the sake of his personal technique, the integrity of his subject to an effect of hallucination, however overpowering it may be, which is not, as it should be, accidental to the artistic circumstance. This is of the realm of psychology and judging from some of his more recent works, produced, it seems, in almost a mood of desperation, Jamini Roy has swallowed the bait always dangling before all artists. How much freer is he in his earlier pictures of the Ramayana series (one is reproduced here), where his subject has helped him, in the manner of our best folk art, to express the grand simplicity of the epic, the *ur*, the primaeval candour of man before history was! Some time must still elapse before modern Indian art, even in the person of one of its boldest representatives, completely dissociates itself from the romantic and subjective overtones. This is one of the greatest drawbacks of having been taught European academism. The Indian of classical times, on the other hand, during the best period, was as jealous of maintaining the autonomy of his objective as the modernist of Europe.

During the most fruitful years of his creation Jamini Roy, however, has stuck fast to his own tradition which is also the tradition of Indian art. Pictures of this period form the kernel of the exhibition and give it the value it has. But he arrived at the understanding of the final ends of art not so much from a knowledge of our classical forms as from Bengal folk art. This inspiration has been the determinant of his individual style, the style by which he will be known; the psychological pictures being in the nature of a *tour de force*. He forsook early the pseudo-Japanese impressionism of the Bengali School. He wanted the clear line and the unabashed colour. He fled from Calcutta to a Bengal village, a flight from overwrought milieus almost in the manner of Cézanne—only that Cézanne with self-assurance and mastery went away to remake his native Provence in the passionate glow of an intense vision, whilst Jamini Roy went to his village to sit at the feet of humble artisans and learn what integrity and fierce sincerity in art meant. These despised artisans, no more artists, who paint our remarkably expressionistic *pats*, though now unfortunately in aniline dyes and in conformity to a debased iconography, taught him the secret of the fundamental rapid line, the expressive contour enclosing the human form in one vital sweep. His work, which is likely to endure longest, is done in this technique. At moments he has left it for experiments in the vertical line, which is also a folk art influence, but he is ever coming back to it, because he has found in it the only satisfying vehicle for the depicting of his vision of the human figure. The travel of the circular accelerated line northwards, perhaps derived from the craft of the Bengali potter, is a fascinating chapter in the history of Indian art. It was a constant counter-balance to the vertical and horizontal motifs in our mediaeval painting. Moreover, it constitutes one of the most fecund contributions of folk art to the charming pictures of the Pahari Schools.

Indian folk art has not yet been systematically studied, in spite of the fact that it is agreed upon by all art historians, that there we are most likely to find the embryo of most of our perfected mediaeval forms. It is also there that all the foreign motifs may still be found to exist in their original appearance as they were introduced into India. I have seen in specimens from localities so far apart as Ujjain and Birbhum in Bengal, one a silver plaque and the other a decorated brick, the well-known image of the Iranian archer on horseback who, whilst fleeing, turns on his saddle and shoots arrows at the pursuing enemy. This Scythian motif, known to us from South Russia and Siberia, was common to all Iranian nomads. There can be no doubt that it was handed down to us by the Parthians at the same time when Iranian influences began to enter from Central Asia into China, for we find this motif in the Han decorated bricks at the Musée Cernuschi in Paris. The conventional galloping horse with the four legs in the air, which Reinach traced to the Iranians, is also frequently to be found in our folk art. In Bengal, because of its nearness to the sea, one is amazed to discover, in the earthen and wooden dolls sold in fairs, survivals of ancient Egyptian models and particularly of the Alexandrian and Naukratian periods. Moreover, we never come across in our cultivated arts the animal motif in its Scythian interpretation, which has been the most important decorative and plastic motif of the eastern world, even for personal ornaments and stuffs, but only in popular jewellery and in those terracottas, which, subsisting side by side with the art produced under court patronage, bear testimony to popular preferences.

In Bengal there are several collections of folk art. The most notable for variety and for the large number of specimens is that of Mr Gurusaday Dutt who, with rare enthusiasm, has got together textile, wood-carving, paintings, pottery, stone sculpture, ballads, during the years when, as a member of the government executive, he lived in close contact with villagers. Unfortunately his collection is not available for study to outsiders, and his administrative work and particularly his absorption in the movement he has initiated for the popularising of our folk dances, leave him little time to devote to the art and literary material in his possession. Credit is due to him not only for having brought to the notice of educated milieus this storehouse of knowledge but for having succeeded in disturbing the smugness and monotony into which, after its initial successes, the Bengali School had settled down. He has helped, with exhibitions and propaganda, to fix our attention on the debased status of the village artists, who once were the purveyors of beauty to the rural population of Bengal. Nandalal Bose, with the selective taste and familiarity with art forms which is due to his being not only a great painter but a great teacher, has also a collection of dolls in clay and wood, beside other art products, from Birbhum and Bankura, the two centres where principally folk art is created till the present day in Western Bengal, housed in the Kala-bhawan of the Visvabharati at Santiniketan. Mr Ajit Ghosh has a valuable representative collection composed of many beautiful things. I have not had the privilege of seeing Mr O.C. Gangoly's collection, Mukul Dey, Dr Stella Kramrisch and Jamini Roy also possess interesting examples.

It is only proper that Jamini Roy, with his urge for simplification, should have at once felt the affinity between himself and the village artists who, unconscious of the struggle in which he was involved, had already solved his problems through layers and layers of experimentation in anonymity and self-effacement. The first thing he did was to change his palette. He left the European and Chinese colours he had been employing for those that are found in nature and are used by the villagers in an abandon of that joy in humility, which many artists have experienced at being brought into direct touch with their native soil. For the yellow ochre he adopted the *holi mati* and for bright yellow, *harital*. The Indian red he obtained from *geri mati*, vermilion from a mercury composition known as *hingul*, blue from indigo and greenish stones, white from *kak khori* and white clay, ivory black from burnt coconut shells and lamp black from the soot at the bottom of cooking vessels. In some respect he differs from the *patua* as he employs the European and not the indigenous goat-hair brush. The villagers use the gum to be found inside an unripe *bael* fruit (popularly known as wood-apple) for the glue, but Jamini Roy employs a preparation, also well-known in India, made after boiling the stones of the tamarind and keeping the glutinous substance thus obtained for a week under water. The *patua* paints his pictures directly on paper, whilst Jamini Roy works mostly on canvas, the ground being prepared in two ways: with ordinary clay overlaid with a coating of white clay mixed with tamarind glue, or with an amber coloured clay mixed with lime-stone (*ghuti*).

Folk art, by its very nature and function, apart from the simple technique and the resultant easy communion with it, must teach many useful lessons to creative artists in search of basic forms. In the first place, it is frankly commercial supplying a definite demand in conformity with a well-established taste. Therefore its message is direct to the eye, without subterfuge or detour. It is a good discipline for an artist to forget an abstract capricious milieu of admirers and buyers and to raise himself to the level of the artisan with all the implications of skill and master craftsmanship included in that word. Secondly, the vagueness of phantasy, which takes its birth in the licence of creation, is properly controlled by accepted iconographical clichés, which, though they offer endless scope for variations, never permit the betrayal of the fundamental form. Besides, the forms of folk art are collective creations, created not only by generations of innovators and discoverers but actually brought into being by several members of one family, each having a definite part of the task assigned to him. The design as a whole is an abiding presence during the process of disparate activity, and the responsibility of each is towards the work before him and to one another but not to any artificial criteria established by critics and snobs. From this we get that quality of honest unashamedness and fearlessness which characterises folk products, so contrasting with the hesitancy due to cultural inhibitions amongst us. The natural results are the significant determined line, the well-sustained rhythm on the basis of approved spatial connections, the undiluted and bold colouring and the total absence of elements incoherent with the theme. In other words, the concentration is solely on the product of art, on the laws of line, light and volume on the intrinsic cogency of the object itself, undisturbed by irrelevant considerations of the picturesque.

Jamini Roy has learnt all this and more from his village teachers. Having placed himself deliberately under the yoke of folk iconography he cannot be accused of striving after originality. But in spite of the restrictions put on his creative talents by tradition his work is for the most part free, individual and unconstrained. A good example of this is to be found in the pictures of the *Mother and Child*, which he has subjected to different treatments at different epochs of his growth. This theme has frequently engaged his mind and that in spite of its being reminiscent of European imagery. He has always held, in contradistinction to the theorists and practicians of the Bengali

School, that a picture is Indian not because of its subject matter but because of the technique and the conception. The earliest picture is a naïve grouping of the mother holding the child's body within the folds of her dress, his face painted in light blue coming up to one of her ears. The covering on the head of the mother is placed rectangularly in the Egyptian manner. It might belong to early Egyptian painting with ethnological traits. The picture as a whole is immersed in softness; the unnaturalness of the features of the figures does not weaken its content. Here, as in all his good work, the features are strictly stylised and the emotional conjunctures banished; the beauty comes out of a shrewd arrangement of the pictorial elements.* But the drawing, in the attempt to subdue it to the exigencies of the theme, is a little too loose and uncertain. Yet, there is a finality in the statement, expressed in an idiom as simple as that of Rousseau-le-Douanier and containing the properties of our popular songs. The second and the best in the series, a black and white outline picture (see Frontispiece) is drawn with a joyous, impetuous line, enclosing the subject in quick circular movements. The rhythm reveals an amazing tact. This is in his most characteristic and felicitous manner, strongly individual, reminding one of modernistic pencil drawings in Europe and, at the same time, of the Kalighat *pats* of some fifty years ago. For instance, the one in my possession which portrays a seated woman holding a flower in a fan-shaped hand with a parrot the back of which forms the shoulder line of the figure, where the drawing is concentrated and restrained, reducing the theme to its essentials. The third picture, which really belongs to the beginning of his latest phase, depicts the mother sitting on the ground holding the child, who is casually indicated, on her lap. The lap has been drawn in the shape of a compressed elongated heart, a shape which suggests the folk art convention of delineating the lower part of the chest. The ground has not been left bare here as in the other pictures but worked with soft spots which intensify the black outline and at the same time give to the picture a deliberate

* See his 'A Woman's Face.'

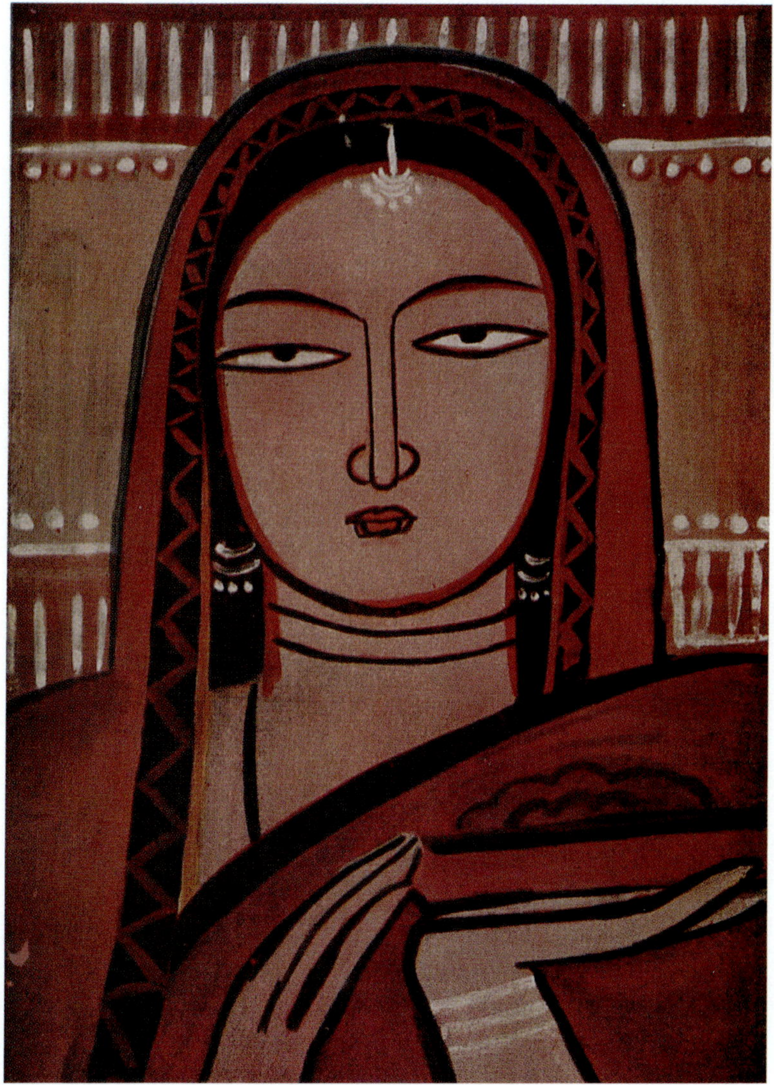

A Woman's Face by Jamini Roy.

plastic quality. This is maturer work and were it not that the painter, to my taste, is being constantly lured towards the descriptive, it would stand as a model for balance and for that trait of his work which might be termed ascetic opulence.

Another instance is of the mother helping a child to cross a pool (now in the collection of the Maharajah Tagore) which was the outstanding exhibit of the All-India Academy of Fine Arts Exhibition in 1935, and to which the judges, with enthusiastic unanimity, awarded the highest prize of that society. The scene is typically Bengali and the subject easily lends itself to sentimentality. But the ingenious use of clear-cut angular lines by the painter and his clean colours have given it the pity and the tenderness of Bengal more convincingly than the efforts at dim portraiture of the *genre* life of the province by the followers of the Bengali School.

However, his deep knowledge of the texture of painting and strength of execution is best seen in his larger wall-panels. Not only are the lines drawn with an unswerving wrist but the colouring is the most exact and accurate for his purposes. They are summary accounts in our folk and mediaeval tradition of the human form. The work is replete with latent vigour and so it is wrong to describe him, as it is so often done, a decorative painter. Pictures of such monumentality may incidentally serve a decorative purpose but they are really pure realisations of form executed to fulfil a disciplined artistic intention with a high sense of artistic responsibility. In these panels the volumes are situated in space in a manner which shows the strong grasp he has of plasticity and yet his figures belong essentially to painting and are not sculptural, a temptation to which a lesser artist would easily have yielded.

In his composition with vertical forms there is a distinct element of the hieratic. However, the greatest delight is provided to the senses by a motif of four women he frequently uses, where the rhythm is as perfectly achieved as in the first compositional essays of man. He uses hardly any decorative ornaments except simple architectural motifs or beads on the person of his figures.

At the present moment, when almost all Indian cultural expressions are in a state of flux, a coherent statement of form by Jamini Roy is of significance. His influence will give bones and blood to the anaemic work which is generally being done today. If he can communicate to the more talented of the younger artists his persistence, his disregard of popular opinion, the importance of his quest for adequacy in art, the creative possibilities within the limits of tradition and above all his technical mastery over definite forms and colour, this exhibition will serve a very useful purpose.

6

On Theatrical Art

I

You will find in Europe in social gatherings, whether they be composed of industrialists, intellectuals or shop girls, that the conversation some time or other is bound to turn to the theatre, and every one has something to say about it. Problems of philosophy, sociology and even literature fill people with a sense of their incompetence to deal with them, but the theatre seems to be an easy enough theme for discussion in which all can participate. And yet in technique the theatre is the most complicated composite of all the arts; for its perfect expression it welds into an organic unit painting and architecture for the settings and costumes, sculpture for the *mises-en-scène*, dancing for its plastic gestures, music for its voices, etc., all these subjected to a well-controlled tempo as the subject matter unfolds itself for presentation. It has been called the most synthetic of the arts, if such a phrase is permissible, just because of this very quality which it possesses of being able to unite in one artistic whole so many diverse and sometimes conflicting components. At the same time, you will see that, preposterous though it appears, there is a great deal of justification for the fact that those who fight shy of intrinsically easier themes, should be discussing it, because the theatre depends for its existence, both as an artistic and a commercial institution, more than any other kind of art, on the generality of the appeal it makes to its devotees and on their collaboration. It is an accepted fact that in all the arts, painting or sculpture, for instance, aesthetic enjoyment produces a momentary identity of personality born of sympathy between the creator and the appreciator, but nowhere is this identity so fruitful as in a perfect theatrical representation, because the art, which is being generated on the stage day by day, is the direct result of the reaction of the spectators and the actors on one another. If you come to think of it, it is conceivable for other objects of art to exist hidden somewhere for centuries without human eyes, except those of the creator, having appreciated them, but for the theatre, where the art forms continuously vanish as soon as they come into being, these forms are all along being moulded in sensitive response to the immediate pressure of the equally important participant in the creation besides the actors and the producer, *viz.*, the reacting public. For this reason a rehearsal, however elaborate, is never a theatrical representation in the real sense of the word. Anyone who has worked in a theatre will remember that trepidation with which the first night is awaited by actors and producers alike. As a matter of fact, as the rehearsals gain in perfection of form, outsiders, friends and relatives are usually let in and for the grand dress-rehearsal, which is the last before the performance, the professional press critics and theatrical patrons are invited. Yet the fullness of representation, the climax of the work attempted, is only attained when it is exposed to the approval of an unknown public. This is an important point to note because the ultimate form which a theatrical representation assumes after it has become relatively 'fixed' as a result of repeated performances, may differ greatly from the original conception of the work by the producer, which at the outset the actors and technicians had intended to realise.

I have used the word 'producer.' It has gained currency in modern theatrical parlance, though people as a rule have a vague idea as to the producer's functions. At the beginning of our century this word was not at all known in countries like England, France and Italy where the traditional theatre still represents the prevalent type. In fact, even today in England, except in those sporadic ventures of what might be called the progressive theatre in barns, mews, and ruined churches, the producer is considered a superfluity, and he is really superfluous because in almost all the theatres the old method of the preparation of a performance under the guidance of the chief actor, who gets his work done by respecting as far as possible the overweening vanity of his colleagues, is still the practice. You will see that the special feature of the traditional theatres is the value attached to individual acting. People go to watch one man or woman and are not disappointed if the talent of their favourite is passably well set off by an intelligent cast which acts as a foil, a passive background. It is for this reason that in countries where such theatres flourish, the public is attracted to the show by means of posters which prominently display the name of some famous actor or actress. Traditional theatres by their very nature must throw out actors of large calibre, who have uncontrolled liberty to develop their mannerisms. Thus, ranting declamation instead of ordinary speech and exalted gesticulation instead of the gestures of everyday life are the natural result. Some of the greatest names in the annals of the modern theatre, actors and actresses of the kind of Ellen Terry, Forbes Robertson, Mounet-Sully, Sarah Bernhardt, Basserman, Salvini and the greatest of them all, the Duse, are the products of traditional theatres.

This conception of the theatre as a place to bring into relief dominating personalities, dates from the Renaissance when man became the centre of all intelligent interest. Neither the ancient theatres nor certainly the more modern ones attach exclusive significance to individual distinction on the stage. The theatre today is not only a place of relaxation but a severe discipline where, subject to one creative will, all the elements—actors, decoration, music, lighting—are infused into one artistic whole. That will is the producer's, a dictator who is solely responsible to the directors for the artistic adequacy of the representation. He sees to it that the essential is not individual achievement, but what is called the ensemble resulting from the team work realised by the interdependence of all the theatrical elements. At the Moscow Art Theatre, the greatest and most important dramatic theatre of the last thirty years or more, the workmen used to ask the producer if certain curtains were to 'play' on certain occasions in the same way, they would ask the names of actors who would be taking part in the performance. Artistic creative personality, however, by its very nature is irrepressible. So it must not be supposed that theatres of the kind of the Moscow Art Theatre do not afford it sufficient scope for expression. What is done today is that the 'stars' are supported and helped by equals, probably slightly less glamorous, but in no way inferior in technique or in execution.

The older theatres are standing on their last legs now. They are being pressed out of existence not so much by modernistic theatres, as there is room for both, and the new revelations of the one are compensated for by the historical dignity of the other, but the cinema which is cheap and which does not demand a high standard of culture for its enjoyment. It is only state subvention which is saving some of the older theatres from the effects of competition. They are like museums, with this difference that they still reincarnate in colourful forms a very high tradition of life and sensibility. Whoever has visited the Comédie Française of Paris with its superb representation of Racine's courteous tragedies or the Burgtheater of Vienna with Frau Bleibtreu, monumental and grandly tragic in Schiller's dramas, will understand that, however, much modern taste be debased and the route to enjoyment cut short with the help of cheap standards, there still exist institutions which respond to the highest aesthetic demands.

II

As we have seen, traditional theatres attach an exclusive importance to the individual achievement of a great actor or actress on the stage; the modernist or experimental theatres set as their chief goal the realisation of the ensemble, or team-work not only among actors themselves but among the actors, the script and the stage paraphernalia. There are of course other differences, but these conflicting aims constitute the most striking feature of distinction between the old and the newer theatres. To my mind, however, in both cases the central position must be occupied by the actor. The traditional theatres would frankly admit this; but the theorists of the modernist movement would vehemently protest because, basing as they do their conception of the theatre either on a new type of appreciation or more often on what they imagine to have been the ancient and mediaeval forms of the art, they maintain that the actor is nothing more than a development in the evolutionary process of the puppet. They would say that the principal end of the theatre was a spectacle, a word used by them to denote a presentation to the eye of an object of artistic texture; like other forms of art, meant to delight the senses and not to provoke incidental emotions. Every theatrical element thus should have equal importance in the ultimate structure of the spectacle in the same way as in a piece of sculpture each line and each chisel stroke is an organic part of the whole. While the traditional theatres give at moments, in a flash as it were, complete aesthetic satisfaction by the accidental artistic combination of the actor's art with his background, the modernist theatre attempts, as far as the limits of the art permit, to achieve sustained pictorialness.

I have expressly mentioned the limits of the art because, as I have pointed out, by its very nature a theatrical performance is a peculiar artistic phenomenon that is in a perpetual state of dissolving and re-making; no one moment is identical in the course of the representation. The traditional theatre, aware of this fact, has considered it an unprofitable labour to harness the fleeting moment to uniformity. The modern theatre has attempted the interesting but impossible task of imposing permanence on transitoriness. That is why the modern theatre is always in an experimental stage; the work done there is of the nature of laboratory work and many of these theatres are actually called laboratory theatres. Setting out to realise the impossible they never attain satisfactory synthesis. Their chief merit lies in creating innovations, and in discovering theatrical possibilities which, if successful, become current clichés in the other theatres. This failure to bring about aesthetically adequate realisations is largely due to the fact that the experimental theatres have not the courage to admit that as long as we do not think and breathe and feel in terms of a collectivist psychosis, as long as we are not supplied with a newer psychological apparatus imposed on us by a totalitarian state, the actor does remain and will remain the pivot round whom our human interest, as spectators, revolves. This is an irrefutable fact. All of us, however, have our archaic and mediaeval moments. It is sometimes even pleasurable to subdue our needs to a romantic illusion of identity with the forms of the past. In such a mood only modern men can condone attempts to repress the dynamic individuality of the actor. Theoretically, the modernists are right; each theatrical element must be subjugated to an artistic design. Nothing anarchical in gesture or tone should break the preconceived plan of the whole. So it has happened that the most successful theatres are those like the Moscow Art Theatre of Stanislavsky, or those in Vienna and Berlin that have grown under the influence of Rheinhardt, which have struck the golden mean by effecting a compromise between tradition and modernistic tendencies. Whilst establishing an ensemble and controlling the aberrations of individual acting, they have given to acting the central position it claims and deserves. Unlike the extremists, being great artists themselves, they have acquired virtue in their work by a judicious use of the plasticity of the human body and by insistence on the human expression of pathos; in a word, on those qualities which are most easily communicable to other human beings. By this they have saved the actor from the risk of being transformed into a marionette, a state to which he is bound to be reduced if, according to modernistic theory, he is treated as just one of the decorative elements of the stage, on the same level as his costume or the mechanical devices. At the same time the actor's vagaries or mannerisms are not allowed to run riot, and an undisciplined firework display is not permitted to destroy the main compositional framework of the representation as a work of art.

You will have noticed that in what I term the traditional theatres, great actors and actresses often rely on inspiration and at their best moments give you a deep insight into their roles, but, at their worst, drag on, eking out their part with the help of a mechanical technique. Each new performance is an opportunity afforded to them for a new success or an unexpected failure. In the Moscow Art Theatre, on the other hand, the standard of acting is fairly equal; the spectator is never disappointed. This, of course, does not mean that the actors of this theatre do not influence popular imagination by the vigour of their artistic personality. If that were so, we would not have linked the greatest achievements of this theatre with the names of Katchaloff, Moskvine, Chechova and Germanova, actors and actresses who, in spite of the fact that they played in a language unknown to the spectators, have been adored by theatre-lovers in Europe and the United States during the period when the uncertainties of the Russian Revolution had made them exiles. Yet, however perfect, disciplined and conscientious they are in their achievements, except in those rare moments when they lose their moorings in the ecstasy of creation, they do not attain to those exalted heights of artistic revelation to which, for example, the great Eleonora Duse usually rose.

You will see from what I have said that as the experimental theatre presupposes a hitherto inexistent responsiveness to collectivist creations on the part of its spectators, it is natural that most of the work in it should have been done in Russia and Germany. I have attempted to show that it fails because it can rarely achieve artistic realisation. But one cannot deny the great influence it is in the theatre of today in which it works as a leaven re-organising accepted values. It is due to the modernist theories that the significance of the theatre as a separate artistic entity has been now universally recognized, for there was a time when the theatre meant either a show house or even dramatic literature. Besides insisting on design in a theatrical representation, a factor which must exist in every work of art, the modernists have introduced that inseparable companion of design, style. No more do we see, even in traditional theatres, the bulging horizon or the permanent side screens irrelevantly decorated with luxurious leaves. On each occasion a new original style for the setting is evolved by the producer according to the plastic possibilities of his theme. Petrified *mises-en-scène*, arranged according to the author's directions that A should enter by the right and B leave by the left, where the sole principle was to avoid collisions on the stage, have given place to compositional arrangements of great beauty by pictorialness being stamped on each evanescent moment. Moreover, the presentation unravels itself in a well-regulated rhythm and does not flounder in chaos. If the theatre is to continue to influence, it will do so only by an intelligent appreciation of some of those revitalising principles which have been contributed by the experimental theatres of today.

III

Having discussed in two of my previous talks the main traits that distinguish the traditional from the experimental theatres, I would like to deal now with the present-day Indian theatre in the light of ideals which modern theatrical art attempts to realise in Europe. As I was connected for a number of years with one of the best known theatrical enterprises of the world, and have had ample opportunities of watching the inside work of almost all the important theatres on the continent of Europe, perhaps some of my suggestions may have a practical value for theatre workers here.

At the very outset I feel it would be profitable to fix our attention on the peculiar nature of the Indian theatre, derived as it is from an age-long tradition; for it must be remembered that in the ancient classical East, besides Greece, India was the only country which developed a theatrical art of her own. Whether this was due to early contact with Hellenism, or to the influence of the Indo-Greek courts, or more likely to the Parthians on our northern frontiers, who were great patrons of the Greek drama, the fact remains that dramatic art, when it achieved its fullness of form in India, had its original characteristics, its own aims and ideals, in the same way as Indian sculpture after it was liberated from the shackles of hybrid forms. Attempts have been made to detect the Hellenistic element in the classical Indian theatre, but so far these have been unconvincing; for whilst a few corresponding details have been traced in the theatrical literature of the two countries, the fundamental ends which the theatre was meant to realise in either of them are as different as are the ends of Indian plastic art when compared to those of the Greeks.

Historically it has been averred that the theatre, using the word to cover roughly all forms of spectacular representation, had its original home in India. This has been attempted to be proved by Pischel, the great German sanskritist, who discovered in our country the birth-place of the puppet-show, which, even today, has such a large diffusion in lands towards the Far East, which were once our colonies. The other theory traces the origin of our theatre to Vedic ritual dances, to unstressed plastic movements and incantations. If either of these claims be correct, you will notice its implications in the manner in which the Indian theatre, depleted as it is of tragic emphasis, has grown, and with this data we can easily distinguish those main lines along which our theatrical sensibility has travelled from those along which the Greeks developed. It is evident that the puppet-show can only evolve into a spectacle and the ritual dances into a pantomime; the actors would form elements in a decorative scheme; the whole theatrical representation would necessarily be subjected to the will of one man, who would be responsible for its artistic worth. The actor's art, shorn of individual contribution, would naturally tend towards conventional postures and gestures. The emotional content would be eliminated as far as possible. An iconography of gestures would grow up, as is evidenced by the numerous treatises amongst us on the mudras or the posturing of hands in different ways to express varying emotional states.

Devoid of a representational background, the plastic nature of the actor's art would be emphasised, bringing it very near to the dance. The spectators would be in the know of these conventions, otherwise the representation would lack entertainment, a factor which in the last analysis is the justification of all works of art. A highly stylised theatrical form would come into being created by producers imbued with the spirit of theatrical traditions. It is significant that the Sanskrit name for the stage-director is the *sutradhar*, the man who holds in his hands the threads, allying our classical art with its origin, the marionette shows.

The Greek theatre, on the other hand, grew out of the Dionysian orgies, from scenes of wild and unloosened passions, from riotous struggles culminating in triumphs. Its main theme naturally was conflict, the conflict of man with fate, a challenge to the inevitability of social values. This is the fundamental trait, too, of European theatres since the Renaissance, from which period the unique pre-occupation of European art has been the emotional crises in the lives of men. The theatre, of course, like all other forms of art, is a sociological phenomenon and reflects social ideals. In India, where, on a bird's eye view of our culture, one will find an attempt to plan out social existence without risks, the element of conflict is eliminated, as far as the nature of the human temperament would permit, for the sake of social harmony. Our aim has been to achieve peace by making it impossible for conflicts to arise whereas that of European culture, derived as it is from the Greeks, is of attaining peace by overpowering conflicts. I would beg you to pause and think on this extremely significant distinction for here is the key to the interpretation of not only our contrasting art but all the other cultural forms. The Indian drama, thus, however paradoxical it might seem, is devoid of the dramatic. Whereas action is the central feature of Greek theatres, ours is lyrical inaction woven into the texture of a pure spectacle. We would define our classical theatre, in accordance with modern terminology, as a lyrical theatre for the staging of musical comedies from which the illusion of real life and consequently the identity of the spectator's subjective emotions with the action on the stage is as far removed as possible. Whereas with the Greeks the *deus ex machina*, the god who intervened to provide a satisfactory solution to dramatic conflicts, was, as the word suggests, a mechanical stage device to relieve the anguish of the spectators; with the Indians he was an inherent deity permeating with his presence the entire representation.

You can well deduce from what I have said that the modern Indian theatre with its attempts at westernisation, is wholly on the wrong track and unless it understands the real nature of the traditions from which, in spite of violent efforts, it has never disengaged itself, it is bound to be an artistic failure. I claim that it is even useless to try to free itself from the past as long as the spectators live under prevailing social conditions and attach the importance they do to age-long ideas of social equity and justice; for, as we have seen, the spectator is as important a participant in the creation of theatrical forms as the stage personnel and properties. If we do not confusedly think of the theatre as we do of most things, we shall have to admit that, retrograde as we are supposed to be, our traditions are more in line with the principles of the modernistic theatres in Europe, who, by the way, make much of their alliance with our past, than of the traditional, which reflect the Greek ideals. I find that contemporary theatrical directors in India dimly feel this, for otherwise how can one account for the unexpected outbursts of song and music in the midst of most poignant dramatic situations or for the garrulity of our librettos. The more westernised among them indulgently think that by acceding to dance and music they are pandering to the low taste of their customers. But this is not so. Our society, which the theatre must mirror, is not so replete with dramatic conflicts as the European is, or what is probably more correct, our traditions do not permit us to indulge in emotional exhibitionism. A visit to the cinema or any of the Indian theatres will convince one that even our present-day dramatic literature, in spite of its seeking after western forms, has hardly ever vigorously brought out the demands of the individual as against the claims of society. The result is that some of us, who have been inoculated with western taste, find the plays tedious, and boredom is the most damaging quality in any work of art. We have not yet, for the reasons I have given, the technical efficiency to be able, without effort, to make the auxiliary themes in a play intensify the central plot. We get lost in a maze of diffuse interests. I therefore suggest that the only fruitful line to follow, till such time as our society completely changes, is to attempt to realise on the stage the purely decorative theatrical picture. Rabindranath Tagore, with the sensitiveness of genius to the adequacy of art forms, have apprehended this as is evidenced by the representations of his students of Santiniketan in which colour, light, music, dancing, stylised posture, beautifully designed costumes and settings make of the show a delight to the senses.*

It must not be thought, however, that the Indian theatre should lose touch with the work that is being done in Europe. On the other hand, it should understand its inherent capacities and inhibitions and then make use of the modern stage appliances and mechanical inventions of order to make of its pictures an artistic success. It is pitiable to see the pride of some of the more modern Indian producers in Calcutta or Bombay for some antiquated mechanical device, such as, the revolving stage or spotlights suited to amateur shows in the European countryside. There can be no doubt that the Indian stage must be technically modernised; the make-up more scientific and beautiful; horse-hair wigs and beards should be discarded; costumes should be artistic inventions. But above all, the producer must not lose sight of the main purpose of his work which is to create a *theatrical* picture. He should never become the slave but remain the master of his mechanical and technical helpmates and always remember the words of the greatest theatrical genius of our times, that the best art is not only the best artistically but also commercially.

---

* I am more than ever convinced of this after having witnessed recently a remarkable performance of the poet's *Chandalika*.

7

The Modern European Stage (1932)

The stage is passing through a crisis must be an oft-heard statement by all who are familiar with the recent trend of theatrical criticism in Europe. Since the days of Seneca there has been no period in the history of the European theatre when this crisis had not existed. Naturally, the seriousness of the malaise has varied. Sometimes it has been merely suffering from the effects of gluttony as during the period of French Romanticism with its abundant productions, at others it has been so near dying, as in our days, that it has had to close its eyes, hoping that the Angel of Extinction might pass by unnoticing. Some years ago the position of the theatre had become so uncertain that there was a fear that it would disappear altogether before the onslaught of the motion picture; in some countries, such as Cuba, it had already been ousted by its rival. In many of the larger European towns theatrical buildings were either transformed into cinemas or pulled down to make way for huge picture palaces. Just at the moment when it seemed that it could no more withstand competition, the introduction of 'talkies' gave it a new lease of life by reminding us of its existence.

The success of the cinema was mainly due to two factors: the cinema was cheaper to visit and provided a better resting place for tired nerves; its products could be multiplied at will and were easily transportable. Thus, whilst the theatre could fulfil the need for the recreation or the instruction of a limited locality, the area of diffusion of the cinema was almost boundless. No barrier of language, not even of illiteracy, stood in its way. Continuous performances, a temporary interlude of silence, the comparative comfort of modern buildings, the possibility of remaining in the dark for long intervals and especially the lightness of the content of the pictures, played no small part in consolidating this success.

Financially the theatre cannot possibly compete with the cinematograph, but it was not this only which brought about the crisis. There is an inherent handicap from which a theatre suffers, its bulk of disparate elements—directors, producers, actors, mechanicians,—which makes it less pliable to changes in popular taste. Not that popular taste has ever authoritatively ruled the theatre except at its worst moments, but it plays a very important part in its material sustenance. The taste of the ordinary theatre-goer is as little an indication of the authenticity or otherwise of a theatrical production as that of the general reader in literature. But by a certain indefinable process there does exist a link between the theatre and its best public so that whilst the theatre influences the taste of its devotees, the public also exercise a control over the theatre. However, the chief difference between the theatre and literature is of another kind. While literature is prepared in the aloofness of a room and is addressed to a nameless crowd of problematic existence, the theatre enters into a direct, almost a personal contact, with its public. The action and interaction of the theatre and its public is one of the most interesting instances of anonymous and unconscious minds contributing towards the creation of a work of art.

In this address I am using the word theatre in its strictest sense. The term is often loosely employed to indicate the building in which a theatre is housed or merely its literary material. It is in reality something more than this. It comprises the stage, the scenery, the script, the actors, the producers, the lighting, the music, even the building and the managing organisation, all forming elements in a living synthesis which englobes them all. It is this synthetic aspect of the theatre which is always implied whenever the word is now used in dramatic criticism or history. The modern theatre is thus a thing apart, living its own individual life of the spirit and body, influenced undoubtedly by changes in taste and technique but not solely dependent for its existence on any one of the elements composing it.

This conception of the theatre dates from about fifty years ago when the Meininger Brothers took into their hands the direction of the Lessing Theatre of Berlin. They were serious experimentalists, who were bent on saving the theatre from that extravagance of declamatory speech, which is popularly called rant. They tried to apply to the art a new method, that of the realistic interpretation of the intention of the author in a realistic setting. It was a theory which corresponded to the tendency then obtaining in the representational arts. Full of goodly purpose and possessed of a serviceable technique, they were not men of great talent and therefore their influence was confined to a coterie, which admired them, but could not give them that encouragement which comes from a wide recognition of a realised work. Little appreciated as they were in their own land, their reputation spread aboard, and as everywhere serious workers had been contemplating the launching of an offensive against theatrical absurdities, they found a number of unexpected allies. In France, a young actor and playwright, Antoine, began training his troupe according to the Meininger principles and opened a theatre called the Théatre Libre which gathered round itself all the literary talents of that period. But the work both in France and Germany was being carried on in rather an amateurish atmosphere of experimentation, which could not hope to hold its own against the technical prowess of actors and directors of the older school. It was at this moment that there appeared on the scene two Russians, Stanislavsky and Nemitrovitch-Danchenko, memorable names which will loom large in the history of the theatre as the greatest masters of stage-craft of our time.

Stanislavsky belonged to the historical dynasty of Moscow merchants who had been as prominent in the embellishment and cultural growth of their city as the Patricians of Rome. During his travels he had come in contact with the Meininger Brothers and, having accepted their method with enthusiasm, had assisted at Antoine's work in Paris. The few leisure hours which were left from the direction of a cloth-mill, were devoted by him to coaching up amateurs, who were members of the Society of Arts and Letters at Moscow. His reputation as an actor of high calibre soon spread and he refused several offers from the Imperial theatres, not only because he was identified with a group and an idea, but also from an aversion for those hotbeds of vanity, slander and promiscuity, which green-rooms used to be in those days. Nemirovitch-Danchenko, an Armenian of Russian extraction, was a new-comer from Tiflis and had, with a series of social plays, impressed with his personality theatrical workers. Being highly cultured and extremely well-read in continental literature he occupied the post of literary consultant to the Imperial Little Theatre of Moscow, which was then, and has remained till now, in spite of the efforts of certain highly-placed soviet dramatists to lower its standard, especially during the early years, the finest type of the academic theatre, the only institution that for its uniformity of standard and classical taste can be compared with the Comédie Française of Paris. Filled with inquietude for the future of the theatrical art, the end of which he felt near at hand in his own theatre, which like a splendid caparisoned horse was tethered too close to a stump and was eating its heart out in immobility, he became obsessed with the idea of introducing into the theatre some reform which would yet save it from becoming a mere object of curiosity for art historians. Strangely enough, though he lived at Moscow, he had not heard Stanislavsky nor of his amateur actors drawn from Moscow society and the intellectual milieus. But common acquaintances brought about a meeting and Nemirovitch paid a formal call on Stanislavsky when he was exercising his actors in a large stable just outside Moscow. They parted and promised to see each other again soon, which they did in a room in a Moscow hotel. They met for dinner and talked through the night in that musty hotel room of their plans for theatrical revival till they were startled to find that the sun had risen and a new day had begun. Of this conversation was born the Moscow Art Theatre.

I have deliberately lingered on this episode because of its importance in marking the initiation of the greatest theatrical movement of any epoch. Though it may seem paradoxical, the theatre they then founded, in spite of its vicissitudes and the opposition to it by the younger hot-heads, remains till today the most modern, if not the most modernistic, theatre of the world. The three principles by which they saved the theatre, and to each of which they attached equal importance, were artistic probity, a strict ethical code for the actors and a sound business organization in which each participant of the theatre would have a co-operative interest. By artistic probity they meant a sustained and conscientious effort by the actor to render not only the spirit of the author but his will. The theatrical décors and properties were decided upon after a thorough archaeological study of the epoch to be portrayed. Inspired as they were with the belief, expressed by Stanislavsky in an aphorism, that the best art is always the best commercial product, they were determined to leave nothing to chance but to devote equal care to the most insignificant detail of scenery or costume. The ethical reform that they introduced consisted of imposing an almost draconian discipline on the actors with regard to the hours of rehearsal and in their mutual relations with one another. This they found easy to attain as they were surrounded by enthusiasts, who were all educated men and women, some of whom had been in the universities. Nemirovitch himself a great producer but not an actor, whose reputation as the creator of the Moscow Art Theatre, by an irony of fate, has been over shadowed by the powerful genius and the fantastic personality of his companion, took upon himself the business part of the undertaking, whilst he was helping Stanislavsky during his leisure hours with the artistic side of the work. They both felt strongly that a new method for the teaching of the actor had to be devised which would liberate him from the clichés and the stereotyped ways on the stage.

The method elaborated by Stanislavsky, popularly known all over Russia as *sistema*, the system, on the basis of all the available data of psychology and the newest discoveries in pedagogy, revised at each step with the advance of these sciences for the last thirty-five years, is a remarkable document of human interest, comprising as it does the practical application to artistic life of scientific theories and their interpretation by a man of genius. His 'system' is certainly the standard treatise on the artistic education of the actor, a stern discipline which resembles the yoga. An indication of its nature may be gathered from Stanislavsky's amazing autobiography *My Life in Art* published at first in America in an English translation and since reprinted in the original in Russia. The 'system,' however, in all its fullness is the property of the Moscow Art Theatre and though known to all its members, with that spirit of solidarity which characterises them, is kept a secret from outsiders. Its underlying idea is the total immersion of the personality of the actor in the role, an almost mystic union of the player with the subject played. Varying the religious image, Stanislavsky says that the actor must die in his rôle in order to be reborn in it. This is achieved by liberating the actor from his personality by a series of what he calls *études*, or exercises, in which the actor gradually forgets his individuality and is transfigured in the personage. For example, in order to play the part of Lady Macbeth, the actress, chosen for her stature and majesty of movement, is not given the words of Shakespeare unless she has already mastered her movements in scenes suggested by the producer but which do not occur in the piece. In a number of *études* she is taught, for instance, to open a door or go to bed or lean out of a window, were she Lady Macbeth, and once the teacher is satisfied with her work she is given actual scenes from the drama, which she enacts using her own words. The greatest care is taken that the fine bloom of Shakespearean language may not be brushed away by a too constant use. Differing alike from the older and the newer exponents of stage-craft, who believe in partitioning the stage among arbitrary groups of actors according to a scheme already drawn on paper, Stanislavsky holds to, what he calls, *the natural mises-en-scène*, that emerges from the collective spirit of the players.

Once a play has been selected by the board of producers which for its contents and its artistry responds to the high literary standard always observed by the Moscow Art Theatre, the actors and actresses that are most suited because of personal and temperamental aptitude, are chosen for the parts. They gather round a table under the chairmanship of the producer, who, in a series of talks, explains to them the historical and social environments of the play as well as the psychological problem underlying it, taking care to interpret as faithfully as possible the spirit of the author, whom he has studied in all his works. The actors then begin reading their rôles from the book without once looking up or making any gesture or indulging in any mimicry of voice or face. After several sittings held in quiet rooms, to which no stranger is ever admitted, you suddenly notice the actors forming incipient gestures, emotion gradually suffusing their faces. These indications become more and more defined till one day the actors of themselves rise from their seats and suggest their interrelation such as will later exist on the stage. The distance of one actor from another, the line of the bodies, the scheme of gestures, the spontaneous division into groups is eagerly watched by the producer as material for the final adjustment of his work, as a gardener leans down his ear to listen to the first stir of life in a crocus-bed. It is at this moment that actors are separated from one another and undergo the discipline of the *études*. The idea is to keep as fresh as possible the suggestions of group interrelations and of the interconnections of the gestures and to adhere closely to the contours which spontaneously have emerged during the rehearsals. When the actors are gathered together again, the painter, who has been in constant contact with the producer, is introduced into the settings, which he assiduously attends, forming the plans of his costumes, according to the gestures and the gait of the actors, and choosing his colours for the scenery with reference to the interpretation the play is already receiving at the hands of the players. One who is permitted to assist at this miraculous birth of gestures and poses is possessed of a feeling of awe, something akin to what one feels when one watches a silent brotherhood of religious men waiting for the spirit to stir before they will move or speak.

I have discussed the 'system' in some detail, not only because I wish to introduce you to the practice of the particular theatre with which I shall be chiefly dealing, but because the art of the actor, in spite of recent protests, still constitutes the most important element in a theatrical representation. The receipt of the Moscow Art Theatre lies more or less at the basis of the education of actors in all the serious theatres of Europe. The meticulous work which I have described, takes long in assuming form, and during the earlier years of this theatre, no less than nine months were required for the preparation of a performance. This contrasts strongly with the hurried manner in which most plays are produced, when a theatre is run, as most theatres are, on a purely commercial basis. The moment the rôles are ready, the play is at once 'released' to the public lest it becomes stale for the players. As rehearsals are held within closed doors, the actors lack that important element of the co-operation of a public that reacts to their utterances and gestures. No true actor ever plays in the same manner before an unpeopled house as he does when it is full. The creative fluid which mysteriously connects the performers with the spectators constitutes an essential corrective to extravagances, and helps to establish those forms, expressed by limb or voice which, in spite of their psychological genuineness, would be merely the raw material of art but never art itself. With this end in view the Moscow Art Theatre arranges three general rehearsals with costumes, make-up, music and settings for the friends and relatives of actors before the play is launched on its first night.

The naturalistic interpretation by the actor, the meticulous observance of psychological and historical details, the realisation in movement of the intentions of the author, are some of the lasting contributions of the Moscow Art Theatre to present-day stagecraft. All these elements are so vitalised in the synthesis of a theatrical representation that one is not surprised when a working man asks of the producer the question: Will this curtain *play* to night, Sir? Apart from founding the art of the actor on a solid psychological basis, another contribution of this theatre

in gestures, can move him. The pathos, which flows from the actors' spirit and lightens up the imagination of the spectators, is the only test by which they can be placed in fixed categories. The artistic power of each actor differs according to temperament, experience or particular aptitude for a given text, but there is a least common multiple which underlies all really successful execution, and that is the impassioned spirit. As in literature and painting, the art of the actor may be divided into the intellectual and the intuitive. The first type was much in vogue before the recent theatrical experiments and after having lost favour, is again coming back to its own on the European stage, especially in Germany. The allegiance of the theatrical critic has been divided between these two kinds of actors, some preferring one and some the other. However, if one makes due allowance for enthusiasms which throw people into opposing camps, both types have their intrinsic merit and the adequacy of the one or the other is to a great degree determined by the content and nature of the dramatic text.

We might illustrate the difference between them by taking two important representatives of either group, unforgettable to those who have seen them play. Sarah Bernhardt, who in her time had the reputation of being the world's greatest actress, belongs to the intellectual type. Endowed with a declamatory talent she possessed a trained voice of a timbre which held audiences in thrall. In all her movements and grand sweeping gestures one could feel the mighty pressure of an over-powering temperament. A long training had given her that self-assurance and almost classical detachment, which comes from the knowledge of the power to control each movement and to link it to others in harmony. Her interpretation of the rôle was clothed in a cultured theatrical accent, in accurately brocaded gestures. The execution was wholly unreal in regard to the epoch or even to the essence of the part but not to the pathos of the author. It was imbued with an element of magnificence, which, whilst her thrall was operative, cowed all criticism. The moment her glamour dissipated, to one inclined to a more personal and a less typical art it seemed that one could almost assert that Sarah Bernhardt was the greatest bad actress of her time. It is probably not quite fair to compare her with the finest representative of the other kind, the Italian actress, Eleonora Duse, who in her group has that place of splendid durability with which legendary fame has invested Rachel. Undoubtedly in the annals of histrionic art no other actress, of whom we have record, has arrived at that utter merging of herself into the rôle, keeping at the same time her artistic personality free and undominated, adding inimitable touches which heightened the spiritual significance of her part as even beyond the author's conception. No finer blend of the intensity of emotions, felt in all the fibres of the body, and no more perfect artistic form, will perhaps ever be seen again. Her voice, her eyes, translucent and yet distantly opaque, the marvellous sculptured forehead crowned with black hair across which ran a braid of silver grey, her tranquil hands to which D'Annunzio has dedicated his well-known play, the *Gioconda*, all distilled to an unimagined degree that quality of the eternal feminine, which was Goethe's quest. Equipped as both of these actresses were with superb technique, what in Sarah Bernhardt was effulgence, in the Duse was a radiant suffusion; what was resplendent in the one was wondrous in the other. Duse's emotions flowed in a perfect formal cadence from a spirit nourished in sympathy and sorrow. The most human of actresses, she touched the inmost chord in the heart of the spectator by an intimacy of feeling and a quietness of expression so opposed to the extravagance of the other.

In the part of Racine's *Phèdre*, one of the finest and most moving examples of the author's classical tragedies, one could well imagine the difference between the two. The queen is eating out her heart in rage and humiliation because of her love for Hippolyte, her husband's son by another wife. In her passionate revenge she has him banished by imputing false charges against him. The tragedy ends with her life. Sarah Bernhardt would interpret Phèdre as a large active woman in whom rage for thwarted passion flamed up into cruel hatred. All the machinations for deceiving her husband into anger would be well thought out. She would make of herself a gorgeous figure supported on exclamatory emotions, strong enough to wield the state and her own destiny in the manner dictated by her untamed heart; her performance reaching the grandeur of her Sophoclean model, barbarous, magnificent and brutal, a marvellous queen incarnate with beauty and passion. When watching the Duse you would feel at once that you had come in contact with the deepest of human tragedies, that of unrequited love and the humiliation in one's own eyes of oneself. There would breathe from her the aroma of hopeless and helpless womanhood in the clutches of inexorable destiny; her plans for the banishment of Hippolyte saturated with the weakness of a lover, who would fain appear strong in order not to be engulfed in disastrous disarray. Every movement of hers would be laden with the curse of love against which her wounded soul could not stand out in defence, in her fevered brain the plan taking the shape of the destruction of love for the sake of love itself. And yet in all her defencelessness of bruised womanhood, one would never miss the queen nor a sense of cosmic tragedy and catastrophe that would even transcend Racine's incomparable work. Such tact and economy of gesture had never been. The slightest emphasis could change it into a tale of domestic squabble. This sure balancing between two infinities, secure in the miraculous possession of unerring technique of both body and spirit, held the secret of that utter tenderness with which she filled our consciousness and experience, while keeping aloof, too fragile even to be breathed upon. With these means she transformed all our preconceived notions of the spiritual possibilities of the histrionic art.

The problem of the technique of the actor, his perfect control over voice, movement and emotions, is of the utmost importance for theatrical art. Technique is the vehicle which serves to communicate to us, who stand beyond the halo of the foot-light, the intentions and the sensibility of the actor. The virtuosity of technique achieved by the intellectual actors such as Sarah Bernhardt, Mounet-Sully, Forbes Robertson, Henry Irving,

Albert Basserman, Vassily Katchaloff, Ruggiero Ruggieri, is of a superior quality when compared to that of the followers of the school of the Duse, who generally attach greater value to the emotions which rise in the twilight of the soul. But as technique is essential to communication, if there is to be a choice between two actors an experienced producer will always prefer one belonging to the intellectual class. The moment of theatrical creation occurs when the disparate emotions are transfigured in a resplendent theatrical personality. Otherwise an actor remains at best an intelligent psychologist. The theatrical quality cannot be divorced from the theatre. A certain attitude of unreality is needed in order to bring out the spiritual reality of a subject with the help of voice and movement. This is a serious charge which modern theorists rightly level against Stanislavsky's tendency to introspection. He confounds the universality of his method with a belief in its universal applicability. According to him anybody can be made an actor. The result is that he sometimes brings forth actors and actresses, utterly sincere in their emotions, but lacking the enchantment we associate with theatrical personality. The moment of miracle, the moment when all is revealed in a synthesis does but rarely occur with them. It would have been otherwise had he followed the Duse's advice given to him in the profoundest sentence ever uttered, not only for the theatre but for all art. 'The secret of the actor's art,' she said simply but with genius, 'is *tutto ricordare e tutto dimenticare*, to remember all and to forget all, at one and the same moment.'

Recently we have been made familiar with a new personage of whom we were ignorant in the earlier theatrical history of Europe, the producer. The word in English is clumsy and a more adequate idea of his functions would be afforded by the term, 'art director.' He is the person solely responsible for the actors, the decorations, the costumes and the lighting, for the interpretation of the intentions of the author—in short, for the artistic totality and significance of the theatrical representation. He stands in the same relation to a play as the conductor does to an orchestra. He has to arrange the massing of the figures and divine the rhythm of the play, leading it up to a climax and then making it recede, which is as important for the aesthetic satisfaction of the spectators as the acting and the décor. In the modern theatre he is an essential figure, for without him the play would be a lifeless mass of episodes, which he vitalises with his talent and to which he imparts an organic wholeness. The theatres of Russia and Germany do not stage plays any more without him. In England, with rare exceptions, the modern idea of the theatre as a place not solely for amusement or instruction but as an art object for aesthetic contemplation and delight is absent and so the work of the producer is done by a coach. Both in England and Italy, lands of great actors but not of great theatres, it is considered sufficient if the intention of the author is fairly intelligently interpreted so as to make of the performance a source of entertainment. In Italy, the actors are trained to this end by the *capocomico*, or the chief actor. The producer viewed as a painter, who on the palette of the stage, uses as his colours, men, lighting, and décor, to form of them an organic picture, has become an absolute necessity. The so-called avant-gradiste theatres of France have all their plays regulated by the producer for whom they use the old term *metteur en scène*, a survival of the times when a stage-director used to 'put' on paper the different places the actors on the stage were to occupy during the succeeding scenes.

No survey of the theatre would be complete if one neglects the importance attached today to stage design, to stage structure and especially to lighting. In the old days conventional curtains, depicting bright-coloured houses and unconvincing fields and mountains used to flap behind the performers. The blue of the sky was so blue that there never was such blue. All this was part of the artistic balderdash that was inherited from the romantics. Till this day we see these backcloths in operatic performances. Their ridiculous unreality is not a wholly unfitting background for theatrical rant or for operatic singers who, holding their hand on the heart, strut on to the proscenium in jerks. With the introduction of realism all this was changed. The stage decoration suggested as far as possible historical authenticity. The illusion of the theatre as a mirror of actual experience was maintained. But realism or even naturalism could sometimes become ludicrous. To take an example, when Andreeff's *Life of Man*, which opens with the cry of a new-born child, was being rehearsed at the Moscow Art Theatre, thirteen new-born babies were sent for from the state orphanage and made to cry. The idea was to register their voices in a gramophone record, which would be set going with the slow rise of the curtain at the beginning of the play. The directors of the theatre were dissatisfied with the cries of the children till one child broke into a typical howl and then they beamed at each other, for here was a convincing theatrical cry. Taste has fortunately travelled far from that period of meticulous application of the theories of naturalism. Now the tendency is towards suggestive decoration; which has the added advantage of being more economical. Thus an arch or some other architectural or ornamental detail may now represent a house. Stage designing and costume, like painting, were subjected to futurist, cubist and imagist treatment. In Russia mere strings and trestles supply a structure for performances. This was due at first to the dearth of theatrical material due to the war and the Revolution. Later on it was adopted as the proletarian's own stage-decoration and became typical for the productions of Meyerhold and of his German imitator, Piscator, the apostle of 'constructivism,' and of the bio-mechanical method of acting in Central Europe. Its success was derived not only from the enthusiasm for modernity of naïve playgoers but because this chance find answered to a real aesthetic need for bare spaces and for the inherent beauty of material, which formerly used to be covered over with plaster or colours. The old curtains are replaced by constructed sets or screens, such as were first advocated by Gordon Craig. One can never forget the impressiveness of the soliloquy of Hamlet, 'to be or not to be,' within high golden walls reaching up to the ceiling made of screens on which the actor's shadow was reflected by lights, in the performance at Moscow to which Gordon Craig was invited and where, in this one picture, he revealed an authentic theatrical talent.

Much of the divesting of the stage of scenery is also due to the fact that, with each day, lighting is more and more taking the place of painted spaces. The invention of diffused lighting for interiors and of easily movable spot-lights for stylised productions, both regulated by a dimming board, has opened up possibilities of suggestion and illusion that the theatre never possessed before. All the moods of the play are now accompanied by what may be called the music of the lights. This is the decorative element of which the producer now most directs his attention. The beautiful skies it casts on plaster horizons, the sense of air it gives on gauze curtains and the contours emphasised by the shadow it creates are quite novelties in the art of the theatre. The future of decorative effects seems now to be inextricably linked with advancement in the science of lighting.

The structure of the theatre is also undergoing transformation. The ideal of some producers like Rheinhardt to create contact between the performers and the audience by allowing the actors to descend to the main body of the theatre and mingle with the spectators has been attempted in the newer buildings. The most important of this is the Neues Schauspielhaus of Berlin, which is a huge circus-like structure, with the stage thrust to the centre from the base of a tangent, making of the inner space a large semicircle. Rheinhardt, the greatest European producer after Stanislavsky, has remarkably utilised this theatre for splendid spectacular performances such as the opera, *Orpheus in the Underworld*, or *The Death of Danton*, where he could throw on the stage and manipulate large masses of actors. The stage itself in all the modern theatres is made into a revolving table on which sets can be arranged from beforehand and changes of scenery can take place with great speed. Also, a system has been inaugurated at Dresden where the sets are prepared on platforms in the cellars and pulled up to the stage surface with the help of hydraulic machines. A less expensive arrangement is that of a number of trolleys, covered with scenery and furniture, which are pushed to the front the moment the curtain drops.

In this brief account of the present condition of the stage some emphasis should be laid on the one factor, which hinders the suppleness of theatrical art and prevents the theatre from catching up with the fast-changing artistic and technical possibilities which are being daily revealed. This is literature, which because of its unpliability, is held in execration by the modernists, who naturally desire each change in the direction of the artistic fashion they foster to be immediately applicable to the theatre. But even stage-designing, which is nearest to painting, is not so supple as in all cases to yield to futurist or cubist treatment. Stylisation in the terms of modernist theatrical art can well do for a Shakespearean or a classical play where there is the element of timelessness but it is impossible to introduce it except in details when the play is one of the realistic pieces of Ibsen, Bernard Shaw, Galsworthy, Sudermann or of the French writers of the last generation. The interdependence of literature and the theatre is extremely significant. While the particular characteristics of a literary work influence the technique of the actor and the producer, theatrical technical achievements in their turn influence the art of writing. Thus, after the first spectacular plays, the Moscow Art Theatre had to change not only the entire scenic plan but also the technique of the actor, introducing those half-tones of the voice and emotions which are its special features, since plays were written for it by Chekhov. The capacity of investing their art with a trenchant and heroic personality, except for a few, seems to have disappeared from these delicate craftsmen of theatrical tracery. In a similar manner, the highly analytical and fantastic plays of Pirandello have necessitated the founding of a theatre of his own at Rome, because the other theatres were not suited to the new technical devices demanded by the specific nature of his works. A new interest in theatrical technique was not long ago evoked in England because of Shaw's *Back to Methuselah*, which was not possible to play in a setting of the usual slovenly realistic scenery. On the other hand the remarkable present-day advance of theatrical technique in America, under the influence of the Russians and Germans, has made Eugene O'Neill write plays like *the Emperor Jones* and *Love under the Elms*. The chronic state of experimentation without realisation of the German post-war stage is faithfully reflected in the works of the German expressionists such as Georg Kaiser. As each particular play demands its own particular stage-designing a modern theatre, in order to live, buys up only those plays which conform to its technical possibilities. Except for doctrinaires, the bulk of dramatists write now as they have always done, all kinds of plays, fantastic, stylised, psychological, historical, realistic and so the flow of literature to the very modernistic theatres is very meagre. The appearance of a play, such as *Hurl, O China* depicting the class struggle of the Chinese masses against foreign exploiters, gave Meyerhold for his Theatre of Propaganda an opportunity of producing a spectacle of real merit. But even the soviet factory cannot turn out many 'playable' plays on the themes suggested by its art high command. Meyerhold has turned to parodying the Russian classics which is described by the soviet press as the assertion of a new proletarian angle of vision, and today, despite some bold theatrical tricks, he is reduced to the tame level of the ordinary producer in any one of the pretentious theatres of Europe. The crisis, therefore, which I mentioned at the beginning, can only be solved when a sufficient amount of suitable literature pours into the theatres and helps to bring out all those marvellous possibilities of theatrical representation, which are being constantly multiplied by recent technical discoveries and innovations.

8

Some Continental Writers (1932)

I

One who has constantly lived on the Continent during the years that have elapsed since the outbreak of the Great War must divine the strong undercurrents which run below the entire social and spiritual fabric of Europe. Even the occasional visitor is struck by strange changes and by unexpected moral reactions but he cannot possess what might be called the physiological awareness of these new forces. There is no use in dogmatising, as is so often done, that these forces have already a definite direction and a programme. In fact, Europe is passing in all the phases of life, through a period of swiftly changing experimentation in which one feels the presence of vitalising elements that have not yet substantiated their claim to recognition as essentials for a renaissance. Their very presence, however, points to a general inquietude of the spirit, which at moments unchains superabundant energy. We are assisting at the spectacle of a world that has lost its bearings and is adrift on the dark waters of time.

In describing the present state of Europe I would not use an extravagant apocalyptic image, were it not that a foreboding of disaster, a sentiment of what the French term *angoisse*, permeates all the works of the moderns, whether in the figurative arts or in literature, in spite of an assumed tone of optimism and cheerfulness. Contemporary European culture hopelessly clutches at every hope, not knowing whither it might lead. It is strongly conscious of one fact only, that change is imminent and must come. We, thus, witness a hankering after social ideals which negate all its democratic and freedom-loving longings but which have at their basis, in the words of the futurist André Salmon, the acceptation of events provided they are on a marvellous scale. It is not to be wondered at if the young are susceptible to the glamour of experiments, which cut across the lives and liberties of millions, but we see the strange spectacle of writers of an old generation, Romain Rolland, Bernard Shaw, Georges Duhamel, Thomas Mann, paying tribute to systems which undoubtedly hold out hopes of a change even if they are utterly at variance with their humanitarian idealism. They are willing to risk all provided the world be remoulded somehow. The War has left behind a trail of bitterness to which the reformers are keenly sensitive. But in their revolutionary exaltation the kindest amongst them would not wince at a similar carnage, only if it were confined within the bounds of national frontiers. Civil war does not appear to hold for them that horror which they experience at the thought of an international war. But the spirit of revolution is as thirsty for blood as the spirit of war. For these humanitarians blood may flow as long as it results in a drastic revision of moral and aesthetic values. They only stand out against territorial reconstitution or expansion. The Great War, they hold, marks an ineluctable cleavage between the old era and the new in every sphere of life. It is true that no event in the history of mankind has so distinctly divided two epochs. But while new political areas have been brought into existence new forms of the spirit have not yet emerged. There might have been, if one were to agree with them, arbitrariness in the reshuffling of political frontiers, but no such phenomenon has taken place within the bounds of the mind, which still clings to the achievements of the past. When even statesmen have to justify their acts by historical reasons, it must be obvious that the products of culture should not be denied their organic attachment to intellectual tendencies of the past. In reviewing the currents of modern European literature it is wise for the critic to adopt this rather conservative view. Nevertheless, one cannot lose account of a new apprehension and a new intention. A literary reaction presupposes the presence of something near and living against which it reacts. This is often an admonition and a corrective and its rôle in the birth and growth of new movements cannot be neglected.

For the extreme flank of modernist writers, such as Aragon in France, the late Mayakovsky in Russia, the group of the Nine-hundred in Italy, and the poets who cluster round Klaus Mann in the *Anthologie Jüngster Lyrik* in Germany, there is no more hateful name than that of Marcel Proust. He is pre-eminently the author of what they contemptuously call passéisme. His most important work, a series of novels, stupendous in bulk, *A la Recherchè du Temps Perdu* (On the Track of Lost Time), was finished during twenty-one years of illness, and was being published with its climax *Le Temps Retrouvé* (Time Refound) till about four years ago. His is thus a literary influence which has been contemporary with all the new modes of expression. There is no doubt that this work in its proportions, so disconcerting to the modern practice of speedy executions, in its themes and their treatment and especially in its pure aestheticism rounds off completely and adequately the pre-War epoch. It deals with the experiences and more particularly the sensations of a man of the world, described in all their minutest psychological detail, which, in spite of the length of the analysis, is deliciously readable. Almost a third of one book is devoted to the study of the different stages in the emotional reactions of the hero, who is Proust himself, at the contemplation of Albertine, the heroine, if there be such a figure as a heroine in this vast conglomerate canvas of men and women, in the posture of sleep. The kiss of Albertine for him was an event deeply linked with all the spiritual and social phenomena of his time. This work has often been called an autobiography. Proust was a brilliant social figure of his time and painted in his hero all the ultra-refined snobbery, perversities, poses, and deliberate inhumanities which characterised the decadence of manners in the Parisian world of fashion of the period immediately preceding the war. But his book is something more than the experiences of one man. It can be called the confessions of the aesthetic Everyman who dates from the nineties. Proust, single-handed, has given expression to all those ideals of exquisiteness in sensuality and vice, to ideals of beauty as an end in itself and to the decorative movement of human sensibility which two generations of Englishmen and Frenchmen had been vainly trying to achieve. The difference between them is that whilst the aesthetes of the nineties gave a great importance to immediate sensation, Proust, like the supreme hedonist he was, took as his material his memory of things that have been. There is something pathetic in the thought of this elegant artist, equipped with all the French gift of penetrative and unshrinking analysis, feeding upon his memory in the despair of an incurable malady. One can discern in his work a clear distinction between remembrance and memory, the latter being a systematised organic texture woven of remembrances. As he says: 'Thus the spaces of my memory by and by get peopled with names, which fall into line, each one related to the other, establishing amongst themselves more and more numerous contacts in the manner of those completed works of art, where not a single touch is isolated and where one part derives from the others its justification of existence at the very instant where in its turn it establishes for them their right to live.'

André Gide, in one of his most brilliant moments as a critic, in comparing Proust's work to the essays of Montaigne, said of him: 'That which I admire most in him is, I think, his talent for squandering. I know nothing more needless, nothing which seeks less to prove.' No social problem, no social injustices ever trouble the spirit of Proust, as he lived retired in his ivory-tower closely pondering upon the tablet of his heart. In the midst of the new sensibilities which were surging round him during the War he remained classically insensible and unparticipating. There is a wholeness and even grandeur in this detachment. No great artist of his type has ever existed who was so unintuitive to his environment and so intuitive towards what was never to return. He could have the presumption of saying with Francis Thompson, 'The world shall glean of me, me the sleeper.' The War to him was an inconvenience and nothing more. So aloof did he live in the deliciousness and voluptuous abandon of his experiences that had he heard the trumpet of doom he would not have stirred to the window, but leant his head back on the pillow mistaking it for a call to a ceremonial parade. As he himself says, he is utterly lacking in historical curiosity. Its place is taken in him 'by the aesthetic pleasure in the search for that moment when everything bears relation to the narrator who says I, but who is not always me.' At another place he says: 'Beauty is a series of hypotheses which makes ugliness shrink, while it bars the road that we already see opening on to the unknown.'

It will be evident why in Proust's deliberate, pure aestheticism the naïve revolutionary spirits find their bitterest foe. His notion of time, a word he intentionally uses in the title of his work, is something static, compassed within the range of a vitalising memory. It is not the modern idea of flux holding inside it the germs of an ever progressive life. To the younger writers, he is the advocate of all those cultural ideals which characterised the degenerate high bourgeoisie. The more galling, therefore, is the fact that their elders and strangely still they themselves are being constantly betrayed into his influence at moments when they find themselves floundering. In the cacophony of their 'masculine' verses or elliptical prose sentences they are irritated to discover how Proust's notes of a subtle refinement imperceptibly intrude. In their doctrinal blindness they do not see that Proust is as utterly dispassionate towards the past as he is towards those who claim to hold the promise of the future. The impassivity of his finely-sculptured Janus face is turned alike towards the road that recedes and the road that leads on. In the flow of time he has captured a refuge and possessed it for his own. No doctrines emanate from him. For all he cares the past and the present might be dissolved in the flood as long as he is safe and secure. He says himself: 'Later I was often ill and during long days I had to remain in the ark. I then understood that Noah could never have seen the world so well as from the ark despite the fact that it was closed and there was night on earth.'

With Proust's aestheticism one may contrast without contrition the other great artistic influence of our days, André Gide, sensualist, communist and seeker after god. His preoccupation in his poems and novels has been to discover the strange possibilities of man seeking the way to an existence in pathos. He has put down as his doctrine 'the negation of all rule, the exaltation of sensual ecstasy, and the annihilation of all that is neither sensation nor fervour.' His great attraction for the moderns, apart from his exquisite artistry and the mastery with which he grapples with his themes, raising them at moments to an unexpected poignancy of feeling, as in his marvellous novel *La Porte Etroite*, lies in the fact that he deliberately sets out to revise the existing moral values, though more often than not in terms of decadence. Notwithstanding, his creed of fervent sensationalism supplies the moderns with a justification for their own disjointed and epileptic efforts at expression. Gide is, moreover, extremely economical and exact in his words, which brings him much nearer contemporary literary products than Proust for whom, 'metaphor alone can give a sort of eternity to style.'

Till a few years ago the calm surface of Gide's genius was ruffled by the breezes, but not by the winds, of social changes, to which Proust had remained so magnificently unresponsive. An atheistic society and the transitional disorganisation of the spirit which would ensue in its wake, the birth of a new discipline based on a negation 'of virtue for the love of virtue itself' was the subject of his last book before the War, *Les Caves du Vatican*, and of his colossal recent novel, *Les Faux-Monnayeurs*, which in its proportions may be compared to Tolstoï's *War and Peace* and in it intensity of pure analysis to the *Possessed* of Dostoïevsky. But it is not merely this which had made him the preferred guide of the literary youth of today. He exhibits a curious combination of moral and spiritual disarray with a certain self-imposed discipline, which lends a quasi-classical formal quality to his works; he unites tradition and freedom from tradition in the framework of a complete, finished work of art. As he himself says: 'Art is always the result of restraint,' and because his material is comparatively fresh and the web is linked with the past he is at once the despair and the model of the young. Besides, the translator and critic of Shakespeare, Blake, Wilde, Tagore, Browning, Conrad, Nietzsche and Dostoïevsky, he alone of the great French writers of today is permeated with the genuine cosmopolitan spirit. Dostoïevsky's faculty of eerie decomposition of the stages of the spirit impregnated with a deep human pity, his divination of perfection in the imperfect are the enduring sources of his creations. But unlike the master he remains always exclusively and deliberately an analyst never even trying to suggest the possibility of a completeness. He says: 'and that what I have been seeking on the long roads is not so much an inn (wherein to feed) but hunger itself.' As a result of this, unnerved the spiritual perplexity, he seeks rest in tenderness towards man, man in the captivity of conventions and yet how supremely free to squander his riches without aim and need. This leads him to the problem of the liberation of the individual from the mechanisation of life by war and the prevailing social institutions. He has thus discovered the most popular theme for the creative powers of the younger authors. He becomes their accepted leader in another way by announcing that the triumph of individuality can only be achieved by the renouncement of individualism. To his followers and imitators, especially in Germany where he is in fashion, this has meant the confining of the individual within the bounds of a mutual-aid collective spirituality. In Russia it has meant the 'rationalised' employment in the realm of art of the creative energy of the individual for the exclusive service of the state.

For him, however, the word renouncement really stood for something else. In art it implied the negation of garrulity, slovenliness, preciosities; it represented an epicurean asceticism, which made him say: 'Everything that is delicious to me is my enemy' or at another place 'I would like to arrive at the maximum of transparency, at the total suppression of my opaqueness.' In life it meant the losing of life itself in order to gain it, a notion much amplified in *Si le grain ne meurt*, the title of his courageous autobiography. Beauty lies in risking, he says. Man must die in sin and sordidness in order to be reborn in divinity. He must be capable of wastage in the Proustian sense. Gide advocates 'the perfect utilisation of oneself in a life of intelligent restraint.' Therefore he says of himself: 'I have lived too wisely till this day. One should be lawless to live the new laws. O deliverance, O liberty!' and in another place 'I have become a roamer in order to brush against those who roam. I am full of tenderness for those who do not know where to warm themselves, and I have passionately loved all those who wander.' He would like to be a hero 'who struggled with the Lord till the latter blessed him,' but in reality he only believes in life because of an almost perfect satisfaction which he acquires 'in the effort itself of trying to believe and in the immediate realisation of happiness and harmony.' It is this deep current in Gide's work, the idea of renouncement, that makes the heroine of his best novel, the *Narrow Door*, throw herself into impurities for the sake of salvation, which has most often been missed by his followers. The elements of the problem appeal to them and not its solution. They are especially attracted by the psychology of disarray underlying it, which makes Gide the most representative writer of the modern intellectuals in the same sense as Proust was of the high bourgeoisie of before and during the War. The authentic intellectual, however, with his indecisions, his vital and complicated moral problems is the bête noire of the German and especially the soviet modernists. But once he has agreed to tread the common way, though reluctantly, even a little way, *poputchik* in the soviet jargon, his adhesion is not neglected as a factor in the task of social and spiritual reconstruction.

It is not by chance that Paul Valéry, the third of the great influences that dominate the literary tendencies of today, should have dedicated to André Gide the celebrated collection of his poems *La Jeune Parque* which he published in 1917 after fifteen years of reticence. Beginning as a symbolist he had come in contact with the overwhelming personality of Mallarmé and his first poems were directly inspired by the master. But very early he found that this practice of verbal mysticism, in the clever words of a French critic, did not satisfy his strivings after an ideal of pure unalterable poetry. Contemptuous of a public guided by vain traditional tastes, secluded and aloof, he was waiting for a new type of consumer of poetical products. Valéry was extremely sensitive of waste brought about by the War and he felt that its trials would sufficiently cleanse man to form of his consciousness a fit receptacle for his verses. He did not hope, as might be supposed, for the emergence of a new man. On the other hand, according to him, his reader should be fully equipped with all the achievements of culture and would give Reason and its offspring, Intellect, their place of primacy in human faculties. The muddle of the War had clearly proved to him the insufficience of Reason in the activity and thinking of man. He shrank from poetical and philosophical intuitivism. If a man of his exquisite culture and scholarship had been given to hackneyed imagery he might have said that he stood for the slow disciplined cadence of poetry, which emanates in the labyrinth of the head, not for the easy flow which takes its rise in the perceptive shallowness of the heart. The logical form was the only worthy framework for the raw material of human sense and sensation. He speaks of himself as a mathematical poet; he believes that 'ornamental conception should stand in the same relation to the specialised arts as mathematics does to the other sciences.' He has laid down with clarity 'that the most general group of our transformations, which comprise our senses, ideas, judgement, all that manifests itself within us or outside us, admits of an invariant.' It is this mathematical factor which he seeks, first in the fecund artistic conception and then in its translation into expression. His is the doctrine of literary adequacy pushed to the extreme. 'The invariant of Valéry,' in the words of a French critic, 'is the capacity to raise oneself to the plane where all the forces of the spirit, artistic and scientific, creative and passive, join in a unique point.' The ideal man, therefore, to him is he who believes in the unity of the spirit to the extent utterly to be able to dominate the vain opposition between the arts and the sciences. At another place he says that a great man is 'a hypothesis of physics, a complete system in himself.' In one of his lighter moments he pithily describes his creed in the following words: 'The things of the world do not interest me except in their relation to the intellect. Bacon once said that this intellect was an idol. I agree, but I have found nothing better to replace it with.'

Paul Valéry has elaborated his artistic theories in a remarkably subtle book *An Introduction to the Method of Leonardo da Vinci*, and in his play about the architect Eupalinos. The choice of his subjects indicates the high appreciation he accords not merely to the masters, but to the master-craftsmen of the arts. He is especially sensitive to the abstraction and completeness of the architectural melody, which emanates from man's brain and invests itself in structural form. That is the ideal he has set for his own art. No poet in any language is more difficult to render into another because his peculiar emphasis is inseparably linked with the almost total etymological precision of French words. To understand his poems, or even his prose, one has to be saturated in the traditions of latinity. A foreigner can only detect the architectonic quality behind rhythms and words exquisitely and deliberately chosen and be content with the almost unbearable gleam which emanates from them, a gleam, which, at times, makes one physically ache.

In drawing-rooms and among younger people on the continent there is at present a tendency to hold one's breath and roll one's eyes the moment Valéry's name is mentioned. His verses are often cited, but the look of blankness, which invariably accompanies the reading, is disguised by one of sublimity. In Valérian circles, which exist in almost all the universities and intellectual centres of France, Germany and Italy, one assists at the pathetic spectacle of a group of people utterly distrustful of one another's intelligence and yet gathered together because of an exalted sentiment of snobbishness. For, as has been said, no poet is no elusive of the understanding which can be put into words, no writer so utterly untranslatable into another language, into another consciousness, even when it is nourished at the same literary sources as his own. It is a paradoxical but not an unusual phenomenon in the history of literature that an author's influence chiefly derives from an understanding of his literary doctrines simultaneously with a misunderstanding of their application in his works. In England as well as on the Continent we owe much to a fecund misunderstanding of this kind of the works of Shakespeare, Blake, Keats, Stendahl, Wilde, Strindberg, Mallarmé and especially of Dostoïevsky and the Russians. If Proust represents the valiant decadence of the man of the world and Gide the creative confusion in the modern intellectual, Paul Valéry is the fountain-head of aesthetic doctrinairism, of a systematised poetic discipline.

I have deliberately chosen three great French writers with whom one could connect the literary tendencies which obtain-today. Not only because of the immense prestige, which French literary productions have always enjoyed in Europe, but because for the last fifty years, since the days of Alfred de Musset, France has been the country of art programmes and manifestoes. No purely literary movement, the very name of which implies a systematic application of a set of creative doctrines, has emanated in recent times from any other country, and this fact was even accepted by pre-War Germany, say, in the verses of Stefan George and Rilke. There, in spite of the fanfare of spiritual detachment, modernist productions have always been dependent on the artistic theories promulgated on the other side of the Rhine, as was admitted by Rilke during this last creative phase. A special reason has contributed to what might be called the literary hegemony of France. Even though Paris is the most important meeting place of international talents, the steady and calculated effort of the intellectuals in France has been to keep their literary sources as unpolluted as possible. In spite of her comparative isolation, due to the deliberate incapacity of the French to learn foreign tongues and the consequent meagreness of translated literature in that language, it has, of course, not been altogether possible for France to keep quite out of touch with literary tendencies obtaining elsewhere. But its cosmopolitanism has been deliberately disciplined to the exigencies of a national literature. Calculation is an element which plays as great a part in politics and the private life of the French as in aesthetic creations.

The works of the three authors, whom we have been dealing with, ride astride of the pre-War and the post-War epoch. Yet, with perhaps the exception of Gide, their literary influences have only begun to penetrate our consciousness since the end of the War. We have especially paused to consider them because at a period of experimentation their works represent solid realisations. It must not be supposed, however, that they hold any exclusive right to be regarded as the only sources of inspiration today. What we claim for them is that their influence has been more general and their literary theories more capable of concrete formulation and application. We must not forget that at the present moment there exist other great literary figures, some perhaps more talented and original than those mentioned by me, who began writing before the War and are continuing to do so now. Admired though they are by the more reasonable of the younger generation they fail to attract a following. They are more like lone lighthouses that imply the presence of life, when the sea is dark; they indicate the rocks that wandering ships should avoid rather than gleaming ports for men to gather in. Gerhart Hauptmann of the *Weavers* is still the greatest man of letters in Germany, Jacob Wasserman of the *Christian Wahnschaffe* the worthiest novelist, and Stefan George of *The Seventh Ring* the most significant poet. In Italy D'Annunzio still continues to posture magnificently in the uniform of an aviator in his lone residence on the lake of Garda, defended by a tiny gun-boat on which he martially saunters forth on the rather exiguous and all too familiar sheet of water, dreaming of Caesar and liar sheet of water, dreaming of Caesar and the Nobel Prize. He still writes his gorgeous unreal prose as in his book of vainglorious introspection, which he pompously called *Notturno* because when his eyes were bandaged after an operation the world was plunged into irretrievable darkness. Though his highly-embroidered words still give a flush of pleasure to a people endowed with excitability and a passion for rhetoric, though his dream of Rome coming back to her own as the mistress of the world, ruling again over Spain and France and England as of old, still rouses in us an indulgent smile at his splendid hallucination, yet no real contact exists between him and the metallic thump to the accompaniment of which that new-old vision is being brought to life in his native country. Happy to be called now Il Comandante, in memory of his tragi-comic military exploit at Fiume, or by his recent title of The Prince of the Snowy Mountains, his decadent simile of horses feeding upon roses has been transformed in modern Italy into rashly-driven motor-lorries along macadamised strade voraciously devouring imported petrol.

In England Mr Bernard Shaw is still adjusting his cap and bells and throwing himself, with that tactless mixture of sincerity and publicity, which he has made his own, into the defence of every movement provided it has the disapproval of the bulk of his countrymen. He still amuses but he is gradually ceasing to shock or to surprise. Receptive as he has remained even now to the breezes that blow, in the same manner as in his younger days he was open to all that then were modern influences from the Continent, Strindberg, Brieux, Wagner, Nietzsche and Tolstoï, he has attempted to include the modern attitude in his *St. Joan*, where even he has been awed at his best moments by his text inspired as it is by the ecstatic simplicity of his subject. But he still remains pre-eminently the artist *à thèse*. He has used his heroine to prove that war cannot be conducted by generals, as earlier he had maintained that medical practice should not be carried on by doctors. He is too imposed in his own traditions not to miss this opportunity of stressing that it was not so much the divine voice in the ears of St. Joan, which impelled her on her startling enterprise, but her simple peasant extraction. By introducing a scene in heaven with a modern man in top-hat and frock-coat, in a characteristic mood of buffoonery, he has attempted to wriggle out of that note of *pietà* forced on him by his theme and which for the sake of his reputation he had to betray.

The older Russian literary camp is divided into two. Of the best known pre-revolutionary writers an overwhelming majority is beating its wings in the void in exile, emigrés principally in Paris. Merejkovsky, Bounin, Balmont, Zaitseff, Madame Gippius are still writing in their old strain to a dwindling reading public. Some writers of a slightly younger generation, such as, Aldanov and Osserghine, are trying to introduce a newer method of treatment and helping to sustain the energy of literary creation in unsympathetic environments. In the soviet camp, of the more important of the older writers, we find Maxim Gorki, aesthetic arbiter of the modern fashion, himself trying to write of the new changes, but in the same accent with which we had been made familiar in *Foma Gordieff* and *Creatures that once were Men*. Official artistic knight-errant of the soviet regime, be prefers, apparently for reasons of health, to live at Sorrento in the pleasant, but doctrinally to him hateful, land of Italy spending every year some glorious weeks of ovation among his relentless admirers in Russian. In Switzerland, in the seclusion of a village with urban amenities, M. Romain Rolland, like a spiritual spider, still attracts to his humanitarian web all the glittering flies that travel to Europe. His publicist and artistic writings of today prove the old dictum of criticism that a well-disciplined unflabby head is as necessary for literary creations as the kind of large and generous heart, which he undoubtedly possesses.

II

The crisis of traditional aestheticism, as we have seen, was already acute during the period which were the incubating years of the War. To one who had been closely following the march of literary events and suffering from a feeling of surfeit it seemed that War, and the destruction it carried in its wake with the suggestion of a new life, was as great a necessity for the outlet of pent-up political passions as for the creative artistic energy. The implications of this tragic presentiment went deeper than the merely artistic problem involved. It touched the whole spiritual and physical existence of the cultured man. The uneven value given to the intellectual against the physical in our lives, which had resulted in deteriorated human types with unbalanced judgments and a senseless detachment from the facts of pragmatic reality had placed the question of education in the forefront of the social preoccupation. He who witnessed the first movements of those who rushed to the battlefield must have noticed how for some the idea of physical prowess in War proved a much greater impetus than the unconvincing slogans that were then being fabricated in propaganda workshops. Involved in the catastrophe, it became evident that those who had a right dosage of physical and intellectual training were greater assets in the combat than those who had developed abnormally in either direction.

Some such apprehension of the problem of the culture of the future lay at the back of the crude minds of those, who in 1909 signed the first manifesto of futurism. In an inexplicable manner, almost in a paroxysm of intuition, the futurists had foreguessed the coming triumph of the doctrine of order based on physical force, which was to replace the undirected and wasteful flounderings of social philanthropy. In the war that was bound to come, they divined the germs of the liberation of mankind from a too great convergence towards intellectualism, which had deified in its temples two meretricious goddesses, Beauty and Sublimity. They were not endowed with great sensitiveness nor could they hear the distant liturgy of events, but they were young and they physically sensed the disintegration round them. The solution they offered was childish, or so it then appeared. They thought that all the evil lay in introspection and in interiorisation, a word they loved for its sonority, by which they understood, if they understood anything at all, the faculty of man to mirror all beauty in his heart instead of throwing it out of himself into action. They were pre-eminently activists, in the palatial jargon of today. The personal, intimate emotions had no value unless they were dynamically expressible; men's veins should be filled with blood and not with eau de cologne. Words in themselves, with their spiritual and aesthetic content, were also useless, or almost useless as media of true artistic expression. They held with Croce that all that came to one in intuition was by its very nature expressible and demanded expression. Therefore from the dictionaries of their tongues they extracted the ejaculations and the punctuations and maintained that these were greater symbols of man's need for expression than mere words. Could they have carried their theories to a logical conclusion they would have preferred, as they sometimes actually did, the bludgeon as the most adequate vehicle for the expression of human emotions. But since theirs was a literary movement, they could not quite rid themselves of the opprobrious habit of using words. So they restricted their application. They preferred slogans to poems, placards to pictures, advertisements to novels and timetables to long tales of travel. Marinetti magnificently declared that it was their aim to free the world of the fusion of two concepts, which until then had been considered indissoluble, *viz.*, that of woman and beauty. They were out to 'replace it with the idea of mechanic beauty...to exalt the love of the Machine.'

Filippo Marinetti was born in Egypt in 1878 and studied in Paris. In 1904 he founded the poetical review *Poesia* and in 1909 began publishing his manifestoes on the new art. He has written both in Italian and French, the bulk of his works being in the latter language. However, his two best books are in his own native tongue, the first entitled *Zang-tumb-tumb* and the other *Five Souls in a Bomb* both of which, though they contain passages of suggestive vigour, are rather tiresome. Marinetti's importance is not so much as a writer as the founder and theorist of futurism. In this programme he has given a hundred characteristics of this movement, which can be summed up in one clumsy word, antistatic. It is amusing, as well as instructive, to know some of them, expressed as they are in his peculiar vocabulary: paroxysm, anti-museum, anti-culture, anti-academy, anti-logic, anti-gracefulness, anti-sentiment, against dead towns, modernolatry, religion of novelty, originality, velocity, geometrical splendour, aesthetics of the machine, destruction of syntax, geometrical and numerical sensibility, *bruitisme* (which may be translated as noisism), plastic dynamism, physical transcendentalism, simultaneity of life, declamation, abstract painting of sounds, noises, odours, weights and mysterious forces, etc.

However absurd at first sight some of Marinetti's postulates appear there is a serious background to them which cannot be denied, in spite of the exuberant disjointedness of his language reminiscent of the patter of a professor of Black Magic. The intuitivism which lies at the basis of futurist products, is a plausible inference drawn from Croce's aesthetic doctrines, which imply that deliberateness should be banished from all art and replaced by sudden illumination, by a revealed synthesis. Croce must certainly have been surprised when he learnt that these hooligans of literature had made of the word, divorced of syntax, the brutal weapon with which to fortify his theory of aesthetics.

Of the followers of Marinetti not one has been able to keep to the word of the law promulgated by him. In Paolo Buzzi, one of his ardent disciples, author of a book called *Aeroplanes*, we see how after singing the praises of machines and velocity he slides into usual traditional poetry. The capacity of sustained insolence, deriving its force from a programme, however much it might reflect the tendencies of the age, is not for any of Marinetti's talented followers long-enduring. He himself, now that he has become a nominated member of the Royal Italian Academy, is beginning to change his rôle of a stormy petrel for that of an oracular owl. For three years before its arrival to power, futurism was the official literature of dynamic Fascism, but now the pendulum has again swung towards the traditions. Soffici, the most brilliant of the futurist painters, has become classical, anti-romantic and xenophobe. However, he still retains his old accent in a new ideology when he says: 'Oh, if I could possess a style which could peel, as an orange, the world of the senses, I would place it before you with its perfume and the juice, which flows from it: if only my words could become as intrinsic and concrete as the thing they signify, and move in the tissue of the sentence like the molecules of a body in a perpetual vital paroxysm, I would then deliver over to you this universe, which stirs within me and which almost suffocates; this universe, limpid and palpitating like a landscape mirrored within the pupil.' Soffici's case shows what a disciplinary rôle futurism has played in liberating thought from the ancient images and adding an element of novelty and almost 'nervosity' to style. With people, however, who do not possess the delicacy of his temperament and the poise of his emotions, it inspires poems such as the one by Palazzeschi, who has now left futurism and joined the band of the neo-Catholic poets.

The Sick Fountain
Clof, Clop, cloc
Cloffte
Cloppte
Cloqlte
Queueueu
Down there in
The courtyard
The poor
Fountain
Sick
What suffering
To hear it
Cough!
It coughs,
It coughs,
It becomes silent
A little, again
It coughs etc.

But not being merely a buffoon the new method does not hinder Palazzeschi from writing true poetry, when he is not fooling, as in the poem:—

Three little houses

With pointed roofs
A small meadow
A thin stream: the Rio Bo
A cypress watches
Microscopic country, it's true
No country at all, but...
Above it there is always a star.

Though born in Italy, futurism has had a world diffusion. In every country of Europe it appeared at the psychological moment when a new mode of expression was most needed. It really supplied young men who were bursting for expression, with an easy vehicle for the transposition of their youthfully energy, if not always of their poetical urge. Nevertheless, integral futurism has never been practised by any of its adepts. Its chief rôle has consisted in setting afloat all those other movements, which end in isms, of which the more extreme literary journals are full and which often differ from one another because of the personal element and because of that natural vehemence, that possesses many young poets, to lead a movement. In a moment of unwonted modesty Marinetti lays claim to the fatherhood of literary movements such as cubism, dadaism, French surrealism, Russian beamism, German expressionism, Spanish ultraism, Yugoslav zenithism and English vorticism. Of some of these movements one is surprised to hear for the first time in the list he gives and their names have not improbably been invented by Marinetti in order to hearten himself that he still remains the sole source of inspiration of modernist tendencies. French cubism has, however, had an interesting destiny and owes its doctrines to Picasso, who first applied them to painting. In fact, most of the movements named by Marinetti belong as much to painting as to literature. Picasso, one of the keenest intelligences of our day, is a Spaniard settled in Paris to whom can be pre-eminently traced, if not the revival, the focussing on the integrity, of painting after the twilight sleep of impressionism. A great and original painter experimenting in all the prevailing manners, he came to a definite conclusion that it was wrong to derive art from the source of our fleeting impressions but from an intuitive insight into the very nature of the object depicted. In other words, his method was to divine the spirit of a thing and to portray it in mass formations or synthetic lines, avoiding as much as possible the representational, however, much the result might militate against our accepted notions of nature. He wished to substitute visibility by vision. He well knew that his theories required a new technique, not that of suffused colours and vague lines which had drawn to impressionism the admiration of dreamy middle-aged people, but the well-drawn precise line, assertive colours and the juxtaposition of masses in all their inherent massiveness. This digression into the realm of painting seemed necessary in order to make as clear as possible the literary implications of cubism. Appolinaire, a Pole, who had lived in Paris and identified himself with French culture was perhaps the first literary exponent of it. He died fighting in the War. During the years 1913 and 1914 his book of poems *Les Alcools* was the gospel of artistic expression which every young writer, possessed of ambition, kept in his pocket and surreptitiously read on the top of buses. To the discipline of his French bringing-up he added an element of extravagance due to his eastern extraction. Surrealism, the natural sister of cubism in letters, persists till these days, though it has latterly begun to recede to the background of literary fashions. Appolinaire's contribution to the doctrine of the new art was clothed in a felicitous image, often repeated by his disciples, in which the deliberate deformation of reality, by dissociating those elements which are ordinarily united and associating others which are habitually separate, was linked with the first creative impulses of man. He wrote: 'When man wanted to imitate the movement of walking, he created the wheel, which bears no resemblance to legs. He was thus a surrealist without being aware of it.' Appolinaire, who was an erudite poet, was apprehensive of the surge of poetical tumult. But he too could not long resist the vengeance of traditional lyrical emotion. Some of his best lines are in the 'Alcools,' such as:—

A family is carrying a red eider-down as
you carry your heart
This eider-down and our dreams are alike
unreal,
Some of these emigrants live here............
I have often seen them taking the air of an
evening in the street
And but rarely changing their places like
unto chess figures.

At other moments, when he is unconscious of his rôle of a leader of a literary movement, he can write a line like

O fils, O-mon fils, plus blanc qu'un lys,

words which cling to the mind for their haunting music. Among his followers, many of whom write in French, but are usually of Jewish extraction like himself, the most imaginative is André Salmon. Beginning his career with such verses as

Then feeling ashamed really
Of being so lyrical,
We offered a cup of white wine
To the melancholic sweeper

he has written real poetry in some passages of *Prikaz No. 10* (*Russian*: Decree No. 10) devoted to the Bolshevik revolution.

O how one should love one another on a
raft which founders:
How one should hate for being nothing
but man!
Of the brotherly gestures God alone will
count the number.
Of the accomplished crimes God alone
will make the sum.

German expressionism came as a corrective to the tendency of surrealism to place sometimes the emotion on a personal plane. It is nearer to its parent futurism, especially in its acceptance of dynamism, physical transcendentness and the idolatry of modern things. In practice it took the form of a 'vigorous exteriorisation of intuitive images' in forceful expression. It is a literary movement, which might be said to be based on blood and nerves, and therefore its measure, both in verse and prose, is often apt to adopt the rhythm of the goose-step. For this reason, the movement became connected with that exaggerated sense for order and discipline, which, in pre-War Germany, had taken on the form of militarism, and, in our days, of the Youth Movement. At less insolent moments, when to justify and strengthen the movement, attempts were made to link it to the past, a sore temptation with most theorists who were used to preach its independence and immediacy, the names of Goethe, Hölderlein, Nietzsche, Dostoïevsky, and particularly of Walt Whitman were cited as the first great masters of vigorous expression. Besides, the aim of the movement being a sort of crude objectivism, it fostered a collectivist outlook, which especially became popular because of the soviet model near by. But the habit of collective action and thinking had been in reality engendered by the experience of companionship in arms, an observation which would make the theorists of the movement rise up in horror. Franz Werfel, the most powerful writer amongst them, had previously written a book in 1913, where he had foreseen the coming trend towards collectivism, entitled *Wir Sind*, emphasising the disseverance of the ego from the raptures of group sensations. The path for this had already been laid by the French school of unanimists, under the leadership of Jules Romains, who in his poems and his remarkable novel *La Mort de Quelqu'un* had laid bare the group reactions of highly personal individuals to one of the most familiar of social events. The soviet experiment was respected for what it promised rather than for what it actually achieved. The necessity of the liberty of the individual almost heightened to an anarchical intensity within the group was a much greater moral need of theirs after the experiences of the War and the old regime than their snobbish adhesion to a purely collectivist system which smashes the individual. The creative leaven to their works was supplied by Gide's ideal of an existence of pathos as opposed to tranquillity. The hero of the new world is man, the victim of bourgeois high-handedness, a conception which loomed in the minds of these writers as a vague windmill against which they were called upon to tilt. Their works are full of abuse of the old system, a favourite pastime of theirs, improvisations of soviet slogans without really in spirit owing allegiance to any definite programme of social reconstruction. Already in 1916 some of the older writers like Heinrich Mann and Rudolf Kayser had cried for 'a dynamic literature, which would be a part of public life, become a source of action and prepare the people for autonomy.' As we have noticed, the chief theme was now to be the experiences and revolt of man in society against social discipline and against the objectivity of the bourgeois legal system. Thus, we find a number of brutal publications depicting the murder of fathers by sons and of teachers by pupils. To explain the psychological motive for these crimes, they would advance the Freudian doctrine of repression. Werfel goes to the extent of calling his novel *Not the Murderer, the Murdered is Guilty*. Georg Kaiser, most facile of difficult writers, known for his 'dramas of shock,' in abrupt sentences, reminding one of marching orders or of business conversations on the telephone, describes, in his trilogy *Gas*, the different aspects of production and its organisation in regard to the individual. In his best known play, *Vom Morgen bis Mitternacht*, he depicts the different states of the mind during twenty-four hours of a cashier, who had robbed his bank of money, indulging in an almost Proustian extravagance of analysis but in such a deliberately ill-conceived style. Sociological themes, such as the waywardness of justice, marriage, liberty, free love, revolts, destruction of the foundations of the family etc. are almost exclusively dealt with in a modernist cinematographic manner by Kafka, Leonhard Franck, Werfel, Bronnen, Hasenclever and a host of less important authors. The theme is revealed and developed with the help of an unprofessional but cocksure application of psycho-analysis.

Vaguely believing that Marx had supplied the best economic solution and Freud the only possible explanation of moral problems, these German writers have produced no one of the stature and significance of Hauptmann, who had also dealt with subjects similar to theirs, only with less insistence and more incision. Perplexed in the midst of their experimentations, and often surfeited with their sociological themes, they turn their hand to any kind of literary trade, chiefly to biographies and to 'improvements' on the classics. Thus, in the manner of Cocteau, one of the shrewdest of French literary snobs, who is so confident that he has improved Antigone by introducing into it a modern interest, they also are rewriting some of the finest pieces of ancient literature in response to the needs of a non-existent schematically conceived modern reader.

In the midst of the political, artistic and psychological chaos with which the Germans have beset themselves, it became a necessity for them to discover an ideal to which they could hitch on their literary wagon. This was supplied by chance by Count Coudenhoff, a young Austrian nobleman of good intentions, who preaches the idea of Pan-Europa, patently influenced by Briand. This ideal was of special attraction to those Germans, who had been made uneasy by the prophecy of the downfall and disappearance of European culture by Spengler in his pseudo-philosophical compendium, *Die Untergang des Abendlandes*. Moreover, as the pre-War nationalistic trend in Germany had educated them to concentrate on the special cultural mission of their country, they felt a thrill of delight at the newly-acquired sensation of international solidarity. With characteristic superabundance of physical energy, German writers in their shoals rashly began visiting Paris, which they generously admitted, after the lessons of the war, to be the citadel of Europeanism. Such Frenchmen as belong to pacifist organisations in their turn ceremoniously but in much smaller numbers returned the visit. Hero-worship swirled round the warriors of peace, such as, Romain Rolland, Georges Duhamel, Jules Romains, Thomas Mann, Croce, Maxim Gorki and others who were otherwise alien to them both artistically and psychologically. In an uncontrolled gush of optimism Leonhard Franck wrote a book *Der Mensch ist gut*. Fritz von Unruh, an ex-officer of the Prussian army, with a great deal of unrestrained exaltation took upon himself the task of embodying the idea of Europeanism, of which he considered himself to be the first propounder, in unreadable novels and extremely dull plays. In their love of Europe, where until then they had been treated with respect but suspicion, they were too anxious to deny their attachment to the East, which had been the historical land of their Romantic yearnings. Collectively they would reach out their hand to clasp the hand of Massise who has trenchantly defended the Occident against the Orient, were they not sure that the latter, the most active spirit of Catholic revivalism in France, would turn his back on them for their atheism. Their mystic communion with the idea of Europeanism was often rudely disturbed by the outbursts of those robust French nationalist, such as, Daudet and Maurras, whose ears still retained the impassioned accents of Maurice Barrès. In certain milieus, however, they raised an echo of sympathy and even of admiration, more for the content of their unquiet thoughts than for their formal qualities, especially in the cosmopolitan literary groups headed by Gide comprising skilful writers of best-sellers composed over the week-end, such as, Maurois, Paul Morand, Pierre Mille, as well as among the bellicose Jewish Edmond Fleg, Kessel, Jean-Richard Bloch and others.

The reason for the admiration of the last-mentioned group for contemporary German literature and of the restraint shown towards it by French Catholic revivalists, who count among them some remarkable men of letters, are partly due to the fact that on the German side many of the most important men are of semitic origin. To some sceptics the attitude of the jewish group seems not so much intellectual as ethnical international cooperation. To make a digression, a significant factor of the European literature of today is the rise and development of a vigorous neo-Jewish school, which is not only not ashamed of its origin but is aggressively proud of it. Because of their independence from territorial patriotism, even in instances where they have been assimilated, the Jews have been more enthusiastic adherents of cosmopolitan and international movements than others. Their names fill the list of the internationalist and pacifist literature of today. What is more, free as they are from an organic sense of European traditions, it has been easier for them to accept and apply the axioms of the new revolutionary creeds such as of futurism and expressionism. In the midst of the hue and cry which they raise round the word Europe one is a little disturbed to hear a piping but insistent voice: 'Let us all gather to save Europe, though some of us may be only recent beneficiaries of her culture, but hands off Zion; that is none of your affair.' Whilst in the day they chant paeans to the spirits of international solidarity in the temples of Geneva or Moscow, at night some of them have been seen slinking under the dark porches of synagogues to pray inaudibly to the God of Vengeance and Righteousness. In France, some of the best known literary names today are those of Jews; this is obviously even more true of Germany, Austria, Czechoslovakia and Soviet Russia.

Beside the sociological and the pan-European themes, there exists a tendency to write biographies. This is chiefly due to commercial considerations, of which the writers of present day Europe, with its economic crisis and the resultant shifting of social classes, show a remarkable understanding. They have cleverly divined the need of the public for an immediate and speedy contact with the subject of the books they read and so have begun writing the lives of great men who, in these days of disintegration of moral ideals, represent integral types. Besides best-sellers, such as, Emil Ludwig with his lives of Goethe, Napoleon, Jesus Christ etc., and André Maurois, author of the lives of Shelley, Disraeli and others, there exists today a large literature of what the French call *la vie romancée* (imaginatively interpreted biographies) inspired by the sensational success of Lytton Strachey. Another branch of literature, with which the book market is flooded, is war memoirs. A sort of morbid interest mingled with pity for the experiences of that great tragedy lived by actual combatants is the secret of their appeal. By an inexplicable chance Remarque's *All Quiet on the Western Front* has had the greatest success in this kind of literature, though it never rises to the fervency of Roland Dorgelès' *La Croix de Bois* nor to the pathetic poignancy of the *Letters* addressed to their homes by the German students, who fell during the War. Henri Barbusse, who originated this subject in *Le Feu*, preaching for the first time in his novel the necessity of a reconsideration of moral values, is too engrossed with his position of a communist grandee, intent on interpreting the new literature of a country, of whose language he is totally ignorant, to find time for essays in creative literature in any serious writing of his own.

A few remarks must be devoted to the Catholic reaction against all the mass of free-thinking which lies at the basis of the internationalist literature of today. For some religious-minded writers the experiences of the War have spelt the return to the folds of the Catholic Church, from which they had strayed. The same longing for order and discipline, that we have been observing, the same disillusionment with the culture of the past and a keen empirical realisation of the futility of human activities have led them to seek refuge in an organisation, the temporal character of which is sanctioned by God. Paul Claudel, whose play *L'Annonce faite à Marie* is one of the greatest religious drama of any time, had already in pathetic prose expressed this yearning before the War. But the real precursor of the Catholic writers of today is Charles Péguy, who was killed during the War and who identified the tension of Catholic mysticism with that of nationalism. In France this movement has produced a remarkable novelist, Georges Bernanoes, author of *Sous le soleil de Satan*, who in the depth of introspection and brilliance of religious analysis, lightened by a deep Christian pity, at moments almost touches the level of Dostoïevsky. Both he and François Mauriac must be counted as among the best novel-writers of today. But, of course, the greatest literary figure of the movement, not excluding Claudel, is the Florentine Giovanni Papini, who passing along the paths of impressionism and then of mild futurism has reverted to the great position he occupied before the War with his Dostoïevskian diary, *Un Uomo Finito*, by writing the Life of Christ, pathetic in its simplicity of faith and rich with the fervour born of religious peace.

Another corrective calculated to appease the turmoil of the spirit among the expressionists is dadaism, a remedy as violent as the disease it sets forth to cure. Aragon, a Frenchman of foreign extraction, formulated the new doctrine, which he derived from Arthur Rimbaud's phrase: 'I have come to consider as sacred the disorder of my spirit.' From the slightly older movements Aragon has retained their dynamism and their passion for sociological themes. He himself is a ferocious partisan of the collectivist theory and is known more in Europe for organised scandals in theatres and cafés than for his writings. He justifies his combativeness by inventing a theory that a blow accurately applied to an opponent has all the content and literary quality of a vigorous poem. In theory, dadaism stands for a more intense expression, for a more bizarre association of wholly distinct elements than has hitherto existed in any attempts at the renovation of literature or the graphic arts. In advocating contentless simplicity it desires to arrive at a new form of barbaric classicism, which neither its admirers, for it has few disciples, nor its detractors have yet seen realised in the works of dadaist writers. They supplement Rimbaud's random utterance with another more definite saying of Paul Valéry's, who declared that 'the human spirit seems to me to be so formed that whatever it does it cannot be incoherent with relation to itself.' Here was a pontifical sanction to all kinds of logical and psychological licence, for that extreme dissolution of all moral responsibility which made Ivan Karamazoff topple into insanity, because, as in Dostoïevsky's memorable refrain, everything was permissible. It seems cruel that Valéry of all people should have been victimised by such an extravagant interpretation of his thoughts. In relation to the dadaists he is like that barbarous heroine who peopled her bed with a monstrous brood born of her own blood. The dadaists claim him as their parent whilst he insistently denies any contribution towards their paternity. This habit of adopting blood cognates in order to swell the numbers of people likely to be affected by their theories, is a common trick with them. They claim, for their own, many who do not wish to be associated with them. They have thus violently assimilated to themselves such divergent figures as Henri de Montherlant, the bard of physical exercises, a writer of the type produced during the late Renaissance, for his famous pacifist phrase: 'Let us push the idea of peace to the intensity of war,' and the soviet futurist Mayakovsky, in his best manner a master of vigorous words which fall with the clang of the hammer, for his weak poem of impressions:

To the right of me Boulevard Montparnasse,
To the left of me Boulevard Raspail, etc.

They seem intensely moved by the geographical direction given by these verses to two rather well-known thoroughfares of Paris, which do not gain in significance by having been recorded by Mayakovsky. In the same way they claim the vorticist gang in England as their own, possibly with the approval of the latter, because they too are anxious to establish affiliations on the Continent. They admire Eliot for his Valérian phrase: 'Pure literature is a chimera of sensation and cannot be isolated from its non-literary sources' and Osbert Sitwell, the amusing member of the Sitwell trinity, for these sarcastic verses:

When Koltchak Murders and Mutilates
His Enemies,
It is justice pure and simple;
Whereas we all know
That the Bolsheviks
Commit atrocities.

They are impressed when D.H. Lawrence clothes his social pathos in the following opening lines of his poem *The British Workman and the Government*:

> Hold my hand, Auntie, Auntie,
> Auntie, hold my hand,
> I feel I am going to be naughty, Auntie,
> And you don't seem to understand.*

Among all the names that they have forcefully enlisted in their ranks they include the fierce band of modernists of Italy, grouped round the journal 900, as well as the classical reaction against it by the Ronda of which the leader is an exquisite poet, Cardarelli. To a student of literature it is indeed difficult to elucidate the common traits between such different writers. The official theorists of dadaism too are sometimes in their rare moments of honest avowal no less nonplussed. However, regaining their self-assurance they startle us with the saying that the purest dadaist is the stammerer, who painfully utters each word. They claim that the sound that precedes the final enunciation is more full of artistic import than the word itself. In fact, the name Dada they have given to their movement is an onomatopoeic form of this vocal exertion. Impudently parodying Valéry's theory of the impossibility of incoherence in the human mind they maintain the existence of meaning in all human sound, however incomplete it may be.

No survey of the European literature of today, however brief and disjointed, should fail to take notice of what may be called the official literature that is being produced in Italy and Soviet

---

* These extracts are taken from speeches defining dadaism at a meeting in a Montparnasse café where the leading theorists of the movement came armed with clubs and belaboured not only their opponents but a chance public gathered to enjoy the cool of the evening. It ended with broken heads and a police report. This document was claimed to be a perfect example of a 'literary' contribution in the dadaist sense. It was also taken to be an instance of pure collectivist creation, since it had emerged from the sudden and violent contact of the masses with governmental authority.

Russia. In Italy the stamp of officialism is not so apparent because it has never been clearly formulated; nevertheless, to any observer it is obvious that all the literary groups there have set themselves the task of justifying and helping forward the Fascist revolution. The first steps in the reconstruction of life along a programme of nationalistic mysticism derived from the prestige of Rome and the Catholic Church, in spite of the disgust that modern Italians pretend to feel for old ruins and historical survivals, needed a literary support, which the modernists supplied by too naïve a joy at the most childish of scientific discoveries. But as now politically the tendency of Fascism is towards a more conservative attitude with regard to revolutions, the wild boisterousness of the 900 has been cowed down by the cold gaze of Mussolini, who has suffered them to play long enough but now desires them to put on clean clothes and arrange their unkempt hair. In Soviet Russia with that stern logic and fanaticism which have characterised the bolsheviks, the literary ideal is dictated by the government. The creative spirit is assimilated to those other activities of man which are forced to work for the state, and is regarded in the same way as any other instrument of production. Collectivism is laid down for men of letters as their only theme. One is at once struck by the contrast between the dilettantism of German expressionists, who long for international solidarity and social reconstruction while helping themselves to copious draughts of beer at Munich cafés and the grimness and determination with which these subjects are thrust upon authors for literary exploitation by the soviet dictators. However, the splendid literary traditions of Russia are too deeply ingrained in the consciousness of the writers for them to obediently carry out all at once what is technically called the *sotsialni zakaz* (the social command). During the period immediately following the Revolution, literature was free and we owe to this fact the remarkable lyrical fervency of Blok, who died of hunger and the ecstatic exoticism of Gumiliev, who was shot. It is true that futurism, as the official creed of artistic expression, was adopted by the government from the very beginning but during the civil war, even the Education Minister, Lunacharsky, a feeble dramatist and a vainglorious politician, had not the time to lay hands upon literature. At this date Essenine, an exquisitely melodious poet, who derived his literary genealogy from Pushkin, was accepted, because of the peasant subject of his verses, his peasant extraction and the freshness of his pastoral images, as the typical poet of the Revolution. But with the consolidation of soviet power more attention began to be paid to the intellectuals, and the birth of a new culture, under the name of proletarian culture, was announced in theses formulated by some of the art theorists of the communist party. At first the definition of proletarian culture was so vague that any writer of proletariat extraction was claimed as furthering its cause. The vacillation of Lunacharsky between intellectual aestheticism and the policy of a new cultural renovation of society, which in spite of his numerous pamphlets and speeches he was too familiar with the old culture seriously to take to heart, brought about his fall and his substitution by Bubneff, a man who till now had distinguished himself only as a recruiting officer in the Red Army. 'The social command' at once changed the face of Russian literature inasmuch as it gave a direction and stability to those authors who were hesitatingly trying to divine the taste of the new rulers. There were to be no more works of art which did not help to carry forth the socialistic doctrines of the communists. Propaganda was to be the function of painting, poetry and novels. The literary tendency was to be 'anti-romantic and anti-imaginative.' The chief merit in a work of art should lie in the accurate description of social and even physiological facts. All the writing was to be as exact a picture as possible of soviet life, but with no disturbing criticism. A mild humorous note might be introduced, as is permitted to Zoshchenko, whose orthodoxy and doctrinal purity is for the present above suspicion, but only in relation to those deficiencies which are superficial execrescences and may be easily rectified. The implication in every work was to be definite and clear, namely, that capitalism contained all that was evil and that socialism in its bolshevik interpretation was the only panacea for mankind. Intellectuals who wrote were organised on the same principles as members of other trade unions and sent out in brigades to study the lives of workmen in factories and of peasants in collective farms and cotton fields. It must be said to the credit of the soviet authors, such as Pilniak, Babel, Fedin, Romanoff and others, that they have been found capable of resurrecting that poignancy and intensity of pathos, to which we have been accustomed in stories of love conflicts, with regard to famine relief, the civil war and sericulture. Here we are face to face with the phenomenon of the indomitable artistic instinct breaking through the yoke of set themes and methods. Essenine could not bear to have the road so brutally closed on all sides but one, and probably this is the clue to his unintelligible suicide. In Russian literature today it is not the best that survive but those who have the most sustaining power, not those who have the most sensitive nerves but the toughest hide. We cannot however deny the force and volume of the soviet output, although we might be distressed by the monotony of treatment and the uniformity of direction along which the literary energy of one of the most artistically endowed people of the world is ordered to flow.

Index